WAITING HIS RETURN

Jesus is coming back....are you ready?

By Candace Brown Doud

xulon
PRESS

Waiting His Return
Jesus is coming back...are you ready?
by Candace Brown Doud

Printed in the United States of America.

ISBN 9781498435499

www.xulonpress.com

Heidi

may you enjoy
this book written by
my dear friend, Candy
Merry Christmas
2015

much love to you,
Shelly

TABLE OF CONTENTS

Dear Reader:

Are you concerned about what's going on in our world?

Are you apprehensive about the future?

Are you frustrated with political ineptitude and empty promises?

Has there ever been a time in human history when the world has seemed to be more out of control? Perhaps. But there has never been a time when we are more capable of destroying ourselves. The anxiety, insecurity, uncertainty, fear, hopelessness, and even despair this produces is visible and tangible. This prompts the questions: Where are we going? What can we do? What is the answer for our world?

This book is a crash course study of the Bible. With today's events in mind, it is intended to give you information to help answer these questions and to give you hope. The focus is on the life of Jesus. Based on Bible passages together with pictures and insights from my recent trip to Israel, we will revisit the places He came the first time, relate them to His return, and see how we are to live in the meantime.

To help us in our understanding, the book is divided into three sections:

Jesus Interrupts History

Jesus Completes His Work

Jesus Changes our Future

Within the sections, each of the chapters, except the final one, has six divisions: The Promise, The Past, The Future, In the Meantime, Personal Reflection, and While Waiting His Return.

I dedicate this book to you, the reader, and I look forward to sharing this journey with you so we are ready when He comes. It is my hope that you will find His peace within these pages because God has a glorious future in mind for those who put their trust in Him.

Candace Brown Doud

Introduction

The Problem and the Promise

$\mathcal{A}$nswers to the problems we recognize all around us and to our future center on one person, a person who left this earth two thousand years ago with the promise that He would return. His name is Jesus, and He is returning to His nation, Israel, and His city, Jerusalem, with the sole purpose of making things right. He is coming to bring peace on earth. This book is written to help us understand that Jesus holds the answers to our troubled world now and to show the great truths recorded in His Word, the Bible, which prove He is coming again.

The Promise of His Return

Before visiting the places Jesus lived His life on earth and relating them to His return, let's look ahead to the promise that is waiting His fulfillment.

Soon after His resurrection from the dead, Jesus physically left this earth and returned to heaven. His dazed disciples were left watching Him disappear when two men suddenly appeared and spoke to them.

The Bible says:

"Men of Galilee, why do you stand here looking at the sky? This same Jesus, who has been taken from you into heaven, will come back in the same way you have seen him go into heaven." (Acts 1:11)

What an astounding statement and what an awesome promise!

The Future We Have to Look Forward To

Hundreds of promises in the Bible refer to Jesus' second coming and a third of the New Testament speaks to it.

The Bible says Jesus told His followers:

> "In my Father's house are many rooms; if it were not so, I would have told you. I am going there to prepare a place for you. And if I go and prepare a place for you, I will come back and take you to be with me that you also may be where I am." (John 14:2-3)

Waiting for His Return

We've been waiting a long time for Jesus to make good on His promise to return just like every generation has waited since He left. But no generation has hated to wait more than this one. We hate to wait for anything or anyone. We even hate to wait the seconds it takes for our hi-tech gadgets to boot up so we can have instant communication, instant information, instant gratification, and instant distraction from the crazy world we live in.

Yet, life is full of waiting. We wait to be born, grow up, go to school, graduate, start a career, fall in love, have a family, get that hard-earned promotion, retire, enjoy the benefits of our labor; and finally, we wait to die.

And every day in between just brings more waiting—for the kids to get dressed, the traffic to clear, the stores to open, deals to close, appointments to be kept, for those we love to come home or call, for the rain to stop, for the sun to come out. We're always waiting for something. Or, sometimes we refuse to wait or give up waiting because what we want isn't happening. But even the act of waiting can be an opportunity, either to take advantage of and learn from, or to squander.

The same is true while waiting for Jesus to return.

Whether we realize it or not, He is the ultimate object of our waiting. Every fiber of our being yearns for the security, purpose, satisfaction, and fulfillment that nothing in this world can provide in a sustainable way. St. Augustine put it so well when he said, "Our hearts are restless until they find their rest in Thee!" God created us that way, with a vacuum that only He can fill, though we try so desperately to fill it with all kinds of things. Jesus fulfills the deepest needs of the human heart. Jesus offers the hope and peace we all seek now and for the future.

The good news is that He is also waiting. He is eagerly waiting for us to recognize and respond to Him *here and now*. Whether or not we respond to Him before He returns affects not only our current well-being but also the future we will experience when He returns. At that time, everything we've done in life and not done in life will be brought under His intense scrutiny. The only thing that will matter is what we did with Him.

Even though the Bible makes it very clear that no one can know ahead of time the exact day or the hour when Jesus will return, we are told we can know the signs and events that will precede this cataclysmic event. Never before in history have the prophecies recorded in the Bible, over thousands of years, been so relevant and recognizable. Even people unfamiliar with the Bible seem to sense that time is running out and the end of the world as we know it is near.

So it has never been more necessary and more urgent to revive our hope and reset our focus, because Jesus Christ is coming back. And when He does— our time of waiting will be over—forever!

Before traveling to Bethlehem where He was born and moving through the major events of His life, it is important to begin with Jesus' claim to be the Messiah. It is foundational to our understanding of Him as the Savior, the One who is the solution to all of our problems.

PART I

JESUS INTERRUPTS HISTORY

Chapter 1

Jesus the Messiah
Returning as Promised

*W*e don't hear the word "Messiah" used much in the twenty-first century. But in the first century world Jesus entered, it was a household word. The Jewish people were eagerly expecting this promised One, this deliverer, to come in blazing fury to free them from the tyranny and oppression they were suffering under the Romans.

Jesus came with a different agenda, however. His purpose was far-reaching and all-inclusive. He came not as a powerful political figure to save a few but as a suffering servant to save us all.

CURRENT RUINS FROM THE
WORLD JESUS ENTERED IN THE FIRST CENTURY

The Promise

The Messiah was first promised in the Garden of Eden immediately after Adam and Eve listened to and obeyed Satan rather than God. That act of defiant disobedience, which is recorded for us in the first book of the Bible, Genesis (Genesis 3), introduced sin into the human race. At this point in time, we can say that sin became part of our DNA.

But what exactly is sin?

We can define sin as any behavior in thought, word or deed that violates God's perfect standard. Sin separates us from Him. So from Adam and Eve forward, we have needed to be rescued, redeemed, saved, or delivered, which the coming Messiah promised to do, in order to have fellowship restored with God.

> **Here's the promise:** Jesus proved Himself to be the Messiah so He will return as promised.

But how do we know that Jesus is this One who was promised from the beginning of our existence to come and rescue us from our sinful behavior and reinstate us with God? How do we know He is the true Messiah? After all, many have claimed that title throughout the centuries. So we must prove He is the true Messiah before we put our faith and our future in His hands.

We begin with the title itself.

In Hebrew, the language of the Jewish people, Messiah means "anointed one." In the more familiar Greek, it translates "Christos." Therefore, we know Him as Jesus Christ, Jesus being His name and Christ being His title. We know about Him through the Bible. The Bible is His resume.

The Old Testament, or the first thirty-nine books of the Bible, prophesies Jesus' coming and tells many things about Him. It tells us He would be from the Seed of the woman (Genesis 3:15), and from the Seed of Abraham, Isaac, and David (Genesis 12:3; Genesis 17:19; Psalm 89:3-4). It also reveals details of His life, death and resurrection hundreds and even thousands of years before His arrival.

The Old Testament prophets foretell that
- He is announced by a forerunner;
- He is born of a virgin in Bethlehem;
- He heals the sick and preaches good news to the poor;
- He is full of wisdom and power and exalted by God;
- He promises the Holy Spirit;
- He is a stone that causes men to stumble;
- He is betrayed by a friend and sold for thirty pieces of silver;
- He is silent when accused and crucified with thieves;
- He is mocked and insulted;
- His hands and feet are pierced;
- Soldiers gamble for his clothes;
- He is buried with the rich; and
- He is resurrected from the dead.
  Scripture references: Malachi 3:1; Isaiah 7:14; Micah 5:2; Isaiah 29:18-19; Isaiah 11:2; Joel 2:28-29; Isaiah 8:14-15; Psalm 41:9; Zechariah 11:12-13; Isaiah 53:7,12; Psalm 22:7; Psalm 22:16; Psalm 22:18; Isaiah 53:9; Psalm 16:10.

The Old Testament also tells us the Messiah would be called
- the Promised Redeemer;
- God's Anointed One;
- King over all;
- Redeemer out of Zion;
- Immanuel, meaning "God with us"; and
- the Lord Almighty.
  Scripture references: Job 19:25; Psalm 2:2; Isaiah 32:1; Isaiah 59:20; Isaiah 7:14; Malachi 4:3.

The New Testament, or the last twenty-seven books of the Bible, fulfills all those prophecies in Jesus Christ, except for one—His return. At which time Jesus, as the proven Messiah, promises
- a new heaven and a new earth;
- He will live among us;
- His kingdom triumphs;
- the earth is filled with His glory; and
- His kingdom is established on earth.
  Scripture references: Isaiah 65:17-25; Zechariah 2:11; Daniel 2:44; Habakkuk 2:14; Micah 4:1-7.

So from beginning to end the Bible provides Jesus' credentials. It's an impressive list that leaves no room for doubt that He is the true Messiah.

Now let's go back to Jesus' time and learn how He began to fulfill all these prophecies.

The Past

Jesus weaned His followers away from thinking in political terms and proved Himself to be the true King and Messiah whose future glory was not tied up with worldly powers or political leadership but with His suffering and death on the cross, a concept that we will learn about as we go through His life. But suffice it to say here that Jesus came as a suffering servant to die for the sins of all who will believe in Him and accept His sacrifice on their behalf. Therefore, His story is unique in all of human history and proves beyond the shadow of a doubt He is the promised Messiah.

A brief overview will help us understand.

After the Messiah was first promised in the Garden of Eden we don't have to read much further in the book of Genesis before reading the saddest words in the entire Bible: that God was sorry He even made us because of our wickedness. So He sent a flood to destroy every living thing except for one man, Noah; his family; and a pair of every kind of animal so He could start over (Genesis 5).

Imagine wanting to start over. But He did. So after only a few generations, God chose Abraham to leave his own country and his own family and go to a new land that He would show him to start a new family, a new people, a new nation—Israel. Through this nation, the promised Messiah would come.

Jesus came from the line of Abraham and his son Isaac, then down generations through the line of Jesse and then his son, David, chosen to be king of Israel. This fulfilled the prophecy that the Messiah would be of Jewish descent, specifically from the royal line of David (Psalm 132:11; Luke 1:32).

God also promised the Messiah would be born from the seed of a woman (Genesis 3:15). So He would be of human origin, but also of divine origin because He would be born of a virgin with no biological human father. The virgin would be indwelt by the very Spirit of God (Luke 1:35). Thus the Messiah would be known as Son of God and Son of Man.

The Old Testament prophet Micah foretold His birth in Bethlehem (Micah 5:2). The Old Testament prophet Isaiah foretold the manner of His coming, the purpose of His coming, and the manner in which He would redeem us—through His sacrifice on the cross—all hundreds of years beforehand (Isaiah 7:14; Isaiah 32:1; Isaiah 53:5).

Therefore, the cross stands in the center of history and beckons us to it as the only means of salvation from sin.

And while many in Jesus' day accepted His claim to be the Messiah and put their faith in Him for salvation, many more rejected Him.

The Bible says:
> Who has believed our message and to whom has the arm
> of the Lord been revealed? He grew up before him like
> a tender shoot, and like a root out of dry ground. He had
> no beauty or majesty to attract us to him, nothing in his
> appearance that we should desire him. He was despised
> and rejected by men, a man of sorrows, and familiar with
> suffering. Like one from whom men hide their faces he
> was despised, and we esteemed him not. (Isaiah 53:1-3)

The Bible also says:
> ...the Anointed One will be cut off. (Daniel 9:26)

In other words, Jesus will be killed.

These prophecies in the Old Testament set the stage for the rest of the story told in the New Testament. It begins with Jesus' genealogy to prove that He fulfills the requirements of the promised Messiah. It proceeds through four different writers—Matthew, Mark, Luke, and John. They would trace His steps on this earth, record His teaching, and validate His death, resurrection, ascension into heaven, and return to this earth.

Their four gospels sound the alarm and shout the Good News from four different perspectives and four different styles so we won't miss it.

Jesus is who He claimed to be! Every word written, every prophecy given, every promise made has been, is being, and will be fulfilled.

Jesus teaches us how to live now so we are ready when He returns. He has a glorious future prepared for us.

The Future

We have this truth to look forward to: **Jesus Christ is the Messiah, and He is returning as promised.**

So the second coming of Jesus Christ will be sudden, physical, visible, and unmistakable.

The Bible says:

Look, he is coming with the clouds, and every eye will see him, even those who pierced him; and all the peoples of the earth will mourn because of him. (Revelation 1:7)

For as lightning that comes from the east is visible even in the west, so will be the coming of the Son of Man. (Matthew 24:27)

The mountains quake before him, and the hills melt away. The earth trembles at his presence, the world and all who live in it. (Nahum 1:5)

On that day his feet will stand on the Mount of Olives, east of Jerusalem, ... (Zechariah 14:4)

As the promised Messiah, Jesus gives us this vision because we will participate in the reality. No one on earth will be blinded to it, distracted from it, or able to escape it. It will be the time of reckoning. The battle lines will be drawn. His kingdom will be established as Jesus initiates a new world government that won't operate at the whims of men and will not shut down under their authority. All nations, all people, and every world leader will submit to His sovereign leadership and stream into Jerusalem from all corners of the earth to honor Him.

The Bible says:

> The Lord will be King over the whole earth. On that day there will be one Lord, and his name the only name. (Zechariah 14:9)

Although there are different views of the timing, an amazing event occurs that all people need to be aware of. Prior to Jesus' actual return to earth, believers are called to meet Jesus in the air. This event is called the Rapture of the Church— not a particular denomination within the church but all believers around the world which the Bible refers to as the Body of Christ.

But how do we possibly wrap our heads around such a concept as the Rapture? It's so lofty, majestic, and indescribable. How can we even imagine what it will be like? The Bible describes it for us.

The Bible says:

> For the Lord himself will come down, with a loud command, with the voice of the archangel and with the trumpet call of God, and the dead in Christ will rise first. After that, we who are still alive and are left will be caught up together with them in the clouds to meet the Lord in the air. And so we will be with the Lord forever. (1 Thessalonians 4:16-17)

At this point in time, believers hear the call to join Jesus and the other believers who have gone before. Together they will enjoy this unimaginable union with Him.

The Bible says:

> However, as it is written: "No eye has seen, no ear has heard, no mind can conceive what God has prepared for those who love him" ... (1 Corinthians 2:9)

This begins a critical time in human history. Many believe (myself included) that the Rapture ushers in a seven-year period the

Bible calls the Tribulation during which time the archenemy of Christ appears. Called the Antichrist, he demands to be worshiped as God and tries to take over the world. At the end of this time, the nations that have always opposed Israel and threatened to wipe her off the map almost succeed. But God intervenes.

That's when Jesus visibly returns to rescue His people, destroy His enemies, and take charge of planet Earth (Daniel 11, 12; Revelation 19, 21). He is returning as the proven Messiah. (We will learn more about this time and these events throughout this book.)

In the Meantime

We live in the most amazing time in all history when two thousand years of accumulated knowledge, scientific discoveries, fulfilled prophecies, promises, and changed lives are proving the truth of the Bible. Each one of us is faced with the question, "Who is Jesus Christ to me personally?" It has well been stated that He is either the most egotistical, narcissistic, insane liar that ever walked the face of the earth, or He is the Christ, the Savior of the world, the Messiah, the Deliverer.

We can stop wondering, searching, seeking, doubting, and denying, and choose to consider the evidence, take God at His Word, and simply believe. In fact, it's far easier to believe in Jesus Christ and all that is written about Him that proves He is the promised Messiah than it is to reject Him and prove that He never existed and that His claims are unfounded.

There's a lot at stake here, because when we believe, we move from death to life, our sins are forgiven, the debt is paid, and the guilt is gone. We are set free to live—really live—because at that point in time, God's Holy Spirit, which the prophets promised in the Old Testament, moves into us and breathes new life in us, the life that was intended for us to live when He created us.

That is the message of salvation, and it is offered to the whole world, to all people from all nations, cultures, tribes, and languages. From all backgrounds, experience, and knowledge. From the seemingly most godforsaken place on earth to the most advanced center of technology. From the poorest of the poor to the richest of the rich.

From those with no status to those with world status. From those with a long resume of good works and church affiliation to those with none.

The invitation is for all.

The Bible says:

> For God so loved the world that he gave his one and only Son, that whoever believes in him shall not perish but have eternal life. (John 3:16)

Later on, this same disciple, John, who wrote this verse, had a series of visions in his old age when he had been exiled for his faith to the Island of Patmos. In one of those visions, Jesus extends the invitation.

The Bible says:

> Here I am! I stand at the door and knock. If anyone hears my voice and opens the door, I will come in and eat with him, and he with me. (Revelation 3:20)

This is Jesus' personal invitation to each one of us to understand that He is the long-awaited Messiah, who came to deliver us from the behavior that separates us from Him, so we can be with Him forever.

Personal Reflection

I will never forget when I came to this crossroads in my own life. I was a young mom. I married at nineteen and had four children by the time I was twenty-five. My husband worked hard to support us. I was a stay-at-home mom with plenty to do. Suddenly I found myself very ill and finally in the hospital with no clear diagnosis and a very poor prognosis. But it was during this time, alone in that hospital room, frightened and unsure of my future, that I heard the "knock." For me it was an overwhelming sense of God's presence and His love convicting me of my need for Him. There was no mistaking it!

That encounter made that hospital stay the best time of my life, because I opened the door and let Him in. To think that God Himself paid me a personal visit and invited me to let go of my pride, to admit

I wasn't as capable as I thought I was, and to begin again with Him. What could I do but give Him my life.

Out of that experience came a compelling desire—no, need—to study the Bible. And I have learned since that true light always leads us to the Word of God. In other words, when His light shines into and penetrates our darkness, we can't separate ourselves from His Word.

The Bible says:
>   Your word is a lamp to my feet and a light for my path.
>   (Psalm 119:105)

God made it so we cannot live without His Word. Anything short leads to folly, futile living, and a fatal ending. We're wandering through life in the wrong direction.

That began my journey of faith. I started attending Bible Study Fellowship in 1972 and retired forty-one years later in 2013, having been a Teaching Leader in a class of up to five hundred women for eighteen of those years. My life is a testimonial to His patience, persistence, provision, and power, as well as His overwhelming forgiveness, faithfulness, grace, mercy, and love.

While Waiting His Return

How about you?

Do you recognize Jesus as the promised Messiah, or are you still looking for another?

We don't have to be Jewish for this to apply. If we refuse Jesus Christ, we open ourselves to all the false Christs who preach a false gospel. The Bible says we will yearn for pastors and preachers and priests and ministers to teach what our itching ears want to hear (2 Timothy 4:3).

Do you seek entertainment or a health and wealth gospel over the lifesaving gospel that Jesus died for your sins? He didn't come to entertain us; He came to save us!

Only Jesus can prove through His credentials, His genealogy, His sinless life, God's confirmation, and over two thousand years of changed lives that He is the Messiah.

While waiting for Him to return, you have the opportunity to look at the evidence the Bible records and make the necessary adjustments in your thinking and your life. You will view life differently and look forward to His return.

Hymns of the faith contain great truths for us to grasp. This one is a good place to start.

My hope is built on nothing less,
Than Jesus' blood and righteousness;
I dare not trust the sweetest frame,
But wholly trust in Jesus' Name.
("The Solid Rock" by Edward Mote)

Now let's move our thoughts to Bethlehem, where it all began.

Chapter 2

Born in a Manger
Returning as King

We could call Bethlehem a sleepy little suburb, located about five miles southwest of Jerusalem. But the night Jesus was born, it was filled with pilgrims returning to their hometown for a census ordered by Caesar Augustus. Bethlehem was about to wake up to fulfill its eternal destiny.

ANCIENT MOSAIC OF BETHLEHEM

The Promise

The Old Testament prophet Micah had foretold this to be the birthplace of the Messiah centuries before He was born.

The Bible says:

But you, Bethlehem Ephrathah, though you are small among the clans of Judah, out of you will come for me one who will be ruler over Israel, whose origins are from old, from ancient times. (Micah 5:2)

> **Here's the promise:** Jesus had a humble birth, but He will have a royal return.

The Past

God had set the stage for His Son's arrival.

Joseph and Mary arrived in Bethlehem just at the right time—the right time on God's calendar, the right time under Roman law, and the right time in Mary's pregnancy.

We have zillions of Christmas cards to paint the picture for us and freeze it in our memories—a weary Joseph leading a donkey with Mary in the last stages of labor. It all looks so innocent, so innocuous, so inconspicuous.

How were we to know that God Himself was about to invade our planet as one of us? How were we to know the cost involved? How were we to know the impact it would have on our world, our lives, and our future?

The Bible gives few details of this most significant birth in history, but the reality is nothing has been the same since. The birth of Jesus Christ changed history. His life has recognizably had a greater impact on religion, literature, art, medicine, music, education, government, individual lives, and behavior than any other. God Himself literally left His throne and set His glory aside to break through our sin-filled world and penetrate the darkness of our hearts. He loved what He had created that much!

So Bethlehem sets the stage for His arrival. But what was it really like?

What was it really like for Mary?

We can't even imagine being nine months pregnant and riding on a donkey over rough terrain trying to find a place to deliver our baby. Our twenty-first-century minds immediately think, "Get my cell phone, call my doctor, and tell him to meet me at the hospital. NOW!" And when we get there, everyone is ready for us, and everything is in place to make us as relaxed and comfortable as possible so our safety and the safety of our unborn child is prepared for and protected.

Mary didn't have such luxuries. She had grown up in Nazareth, a little town about ninety miles north of Bethlehem. According to the custom of the day, her parents had arranged for her to marry Joseph, who was also from Nazareth. And like any young couple in that time and place, they were just looking forward to a happy, quiet, and modest life there. They would be surrounded by family and friends, where they could raise their own family and grow old together.

But all that changed one day.

The Bible says:

… God sent the angel Gabriel to Nazareth, a town in Galilee, to a virgin pledged to be married to a man named Joseph, a descendant of David. The virgin's name was Mary. The angel went to her and said, "Greetings, you who are highly favored! The Lord is with you."

Mary was greatly troubled at his words and wondered what kind of greeting this might be.

But the angel said to her, "Do not be afraid, Mary, you have found favor with God. You will be with child and give birth to a son, and you are to give him the name Jesus. He will be great and will be called the Son of the Most High. The Lord God will give him the throne of his father David, and he will reign over the house of Jacob forever; his kingdom will never end."

"How will this be," Mary asked the angel, "since I am a virgin?"

The angel answered, "The Holy Spirit will come upon you, and the power of the Most High will overshadow you. So the holy one to be born will be called the Son of God. Even Elizabeth your relative is going to have a child in her old age, and she who was said to be barren is in her sixth month. For nothing is impossible with God."

"I am the Lord's servant," Mary answered. "May it be to me as you have said." Then the angel left her. (Luke 1:26-38)

It was just as the angel said, but not until Mary said yes! Not until she put aside her own plans, her own dreams, her own understanding, her own reputation, her own security with a devoted husband and supportive family, her own position as a young Jewish woman, and, indeed, her own life.

After all, who is going to really believe that an angel visited her? Or that she would become pregnant without having sex? Or that her child would be great, even called the Son of God? Or that He would inherit the throne of David and reign over Israel, and that His kingdom would never end? In her world, such talk guaranteed a sentence of death by stoning.

But Mary didn't hesitate, except to ask the logical question, "How can this be since I am a virgin?" Even though there is no way she could have understood everything the angel told her in response, she never stopped to consider the consequences. She heard the messenger, received the message, accepted the call, believed, and never looked back.

But can't you just hear the gossip? "Are you serious? What's gotten into Mary? She's gone off the deep end. She's delusional. She must have some serious PMS. And poor Joseph! The best thing for him to do is end it now. She's only going to get worse!"

Whatever she was hearing, Mary turned a deaf ear. In fact, she couldn't contain her joy and immediately ran to her relative Elizabeth and poured out her heart in praise for what God was doing.

The Bible says **Mary said:**

My soul glorifies the Lord and my spirit rejoices in God my Savior, for he has been mindful of the humble state of his servant.

From now on all generations shall call me blessed, for the Mighty One has done great things for me—holy is his name.

His mercy extends to those who fear him, from generation to generation.

He has performed mighty deeds with his arm; he has scattered those who are proud in their inmost thoughts.

He has brought down rulers from their thrones but has lifted up the humble.

He has filled the hungry with good things but has sent the rich away empty.

He has helped his servant Israel, remembering to be merciful to Abraham and his descendants forever, even as he said to our fathers. (Luke 1:46-55)

But now, here she is, nine months later—dirty, exhausted, and sore after the long journey with no hotel and spa reservation to prepare her for this great event. No hospital waiting to welcome her and deliver her baby in a sterile environment. Not even a room in the local inn where she could have some privacy and await her son's arrival.

Yet we don't hear a word of complaint. No "Where are you God when I need you the most?" or "Is this the thanks I get?" or "What's in this for me?" Only compliance, submission, acceptance, and total surrender of her will and her rights to Almighty God.

What about Joseph—what was it like for him?

The Bible has little to say about this young man God chose to be the foster father of His Son. But it does give us the most crucial information, his genealogy, because it traces his lineage back to David and clear back to Abraham. This proves his own Jewish descent and requires him to be in Bethlehem for the census precisely when Mary is due to give birth—just as the prophecy had foretold.

So at this point, Joseph and Mary are engaged to be married and suddenly she's pregnant, not by another man, but by the Holy Spirit of God. And now she is ready to deliver.

The Bible says:

> This is how the birth of Jesus Christ came about: His
> mother Mary was pledged to be married to Joseph, but
> before they came together, she was found to be with
> child through the Holy Spirit. Because Joseph her hus-
> band was a righteous man and did not want to expose her
> to public disgrace, he had in mind to divorce her quietly.
> (Matthew 1:18-19)

What does it mean that Joseph was a righteous man? The word
righteous means simply to do the right thing. Joseph did the right
thing. He didn't laugh in Mary's face and humiliate her. He didn't
say, "I didn't sign up for this" and bolt! He didn't try to save his own
face and reputation by making her a public spectacle and spreading
ugly rumors. His first thought, instead, was to divorce Mary quietly
to protect her and this unborn holy child that wasn't even his. Then
he heard from God.

The Bible says:

> But after he considered this, an angel of the Lord appeared
> to him in a dream and said, "Joseph son of David, do not
> be afraid to take Mary home as your wife, because what
> is conceived in her is from the Holy Spirit. She will give
> birth to a son, and you are to give him the name Jesus,
> because he will save his people from their sins."
>
> All this took place to fulfill what the Lord had said
> through the prophet: "The virgin will be with child
> and will give birth to a son, and they will call him
> Immanuel"—which means, "God with us."
>
> When Joseph woke up, he did what the angel of the
> Lord had commanded him and took Mary home as his
> wife. But he had no union with her until she gave birth to a
> son. And he gave him the name Jesus. (Matthew 1:20-25)

Joseph did the right thing, when it would have been so easy and
so understandable to do what seemed best for him. Think how easy
it would have been to bow out of her life and run away and start over

with someone else. And who would really blame him? But he didn't!
Instead, he displayed the character traits that made him God's pick
to raise His Son. Imagine waking up and realizing that God wanted
you to step in and assume that responsibility! But like Mary, Joseph
didn't hesitate.

Meanwhile, what about the innkeeper?

Imagine what it was like for him, as hundreds of people poured
into Bethlehem to register for the census. It must have been total
chaos as everyone was looking for a place to stay. And even though
he must have felt sorry for this desperate young man begging him
for a room for his very pregnant wife, the innkeeper had nothing to
offer them. That is, until he remembered the little stable out back,
which Joseph gratefully accepted.

The Bible says:

> While they were there, the time came for the baby to be
> born, and she gave birth to her firstborn, a son. She wrapped
> him in cloths and placed him in a manger, because there
> was no room for them in the inn. (Luke 2:6-7)

And so it was that the Old Testament prophet Isaiah's prophecy
was fulfilled: The virgin will be with child and will give birth to a
son, and will call him Immanuel (Isaiah 7:14).

Churches around the world reenact this scene every Christmas.
The story is told, children act it out, choirs sing, and everyone joins
in the familiar carols: "It Came upon a Midnight Clear"; "O Little
Town of Bethlehem"; "Away in a Manger." The lights are dimmed,
the candles are lit, and we remember that night. It all seems so beautiful, so serene, and so peaceful. So from "Silent Night," we sing,
"Sleep in heavenly peace." We blow out our candles and go our way,
feeling a little more sure that we can.

But that night was anything but peaceful. The birth of Jesus
Christ electrified the world. News of His birth spread faster than we
can tweet. It traveled from heaven to earth in a nanosecond.

The Bible says some shepherds were the first to hear:
> And there were shepherds living out in the fields nearby, keeping watch over their flocks at night. An angel of the Lord appeared to them, and the glory of the Lord shone around them and they were terrified.
>
> But the angel said to them, "Do not be afraid, I bring you good news of great joy that will be for all the people. Today in the town of David a Savior has been born to you; he is Christ the Lord. This will be a sign to you: you will find a baby wrapped in cloths and lying in a manger." (Luke 2:8-12)

Heaven itself exploded.
> Suddenly a great company of the heavenly host appeared with the angel, praising God and saying, "GLORY TO GOD IN THE HIGHEST, AND ON EARTH PEACE TO MEN ON WHOM HIS FAVOR RESTS." (Luke 2:13-14)

Immediately, the shepherds looked at each other and said, "Let's go!"
> "Let's go to Bethlehem and see this thing that has happened, which the Lord has told us about."
>
> So they hurried off and found Mary and Joseph, and the baby, who was lying in the manger. When they had seen him, they spread the word concerning what had been told them about this child, and all who heard it were amazed at what the shepherds said to them. But Mary treasured up all these things and pondered them in her heart.
>
> The shepherds returned, glorifying and praising God for all the things they had heard and seen, which were just as they had been told. (Luke 2:15-20)

These shepherds were forever changed by Jesus' birth. God recognized their poor status before men and changed their image. They went their way with their heads held high and their message clear: The Messiah is here and we saw Him!

Today the Church of the Nativity sits on the very spot where it is thought that Jesus was born.

CHURCH OF THE NATIVITY

INSIDE CHURCH OF THE NATIVITY

It is a very sacred site in the Christian faith and one of the world's oldest surviving churches, but it was just a simple stable then. Even without Twitter, texting, or cell phones, wise men coming from the east knew about His birth.

The Bible says:

> After Jesus was born in Bethlehem in Judea, during the time of King Herod, Magi from the east came to Jerusalem and asked, "Where is the one who has been born king of the Jews? We saw his star in the east and have come to worship him." (Matthew 2: 1-2)

These Magi, also called wise men, were astrologers, perhaps from Babylon, Persia, or the Arabian Desert. So when they saw the star, they were curious. They knew it was unique. So they pursued it and came to worship Jesus. The Bible tells us they presented Him with costly gifts: gold, frankincense, and myrrh.

Meanwhile, the news spread to King Herod and everyone in Jerusalem, including the Jewish religious leaders, who put two and two together and remembered the prophecy from the Old Testament prophet Micah.

The Bible says:

> But you, Bethlehem Ephrathah, though you are small among the clans of Judah, out of you will come for me one who will be a ruler over Israel, whose origins are from old, from ancient times." (Micah 5:2)

But instead of rushing out to welcome the long-promised Messiah, people were agitated, troubled, disturbed, and threatened. The whole city was thrown into confusion.

So once again, an angel appears to Joseph and warns him to take Mary and his newborn son and flee to Egypt, because Herod would try to end Jesus' life by killing all the baby boys under two years of age in Bethlehem and the surrounding area.

The Bible records the indescribable grief prophesied by the Old Testament prophet, Jeremiah:
> "A voice is heard in Ramah, weeping and great mourning,
> Rachel weeping for her children and refusing to be
> comforted, because they are no more." (Matthew 2:18
> [Jeremiah 31:15])

Every Jewish family was affected, as sons, grandsons, brothers, nephews, and cousins were slaughtered by a jealous king who refused to open his heart, learn the truth, and worship the real King. So nothing was peaceful about the birth of Jesus Christ.

Why did God choose such a harsh and humble beginning for Himself to be born when we know there's nothing like welcoming a new baby into this world? We look forward to it with great joy and anticipation. We decorate the room, wash the tiny clothes, and do all the right things to ensure that he or she will have a wonderful beginning in this life. Why didn't God see to it that Jesus would have such a warm welcome? He knew all He would face later. Why didn't He at least see to it that He'd have a royal birth? We know how much fun that is. We rejoice over the fuss: the royal announcement, the trumpet, the crowds of happy people, and the beaming couple taking their precious prince home to the waiting palace. Why would God allow His Son to experience anything less?

The Bible answers that question for us and tells us that He brings down the proud and exalts the lowly (1 Corinthians 1:27). He was giving us a graphic example. Jesus' birth turned the world upside down, or should we say, "right side up."

The Bible says:
> "For my thoughts are not your thoughts, neither are your
> ways my ways," declares the Lord. (Isaiah 55:8)

Because of Joseph's dream, the family did not return to Bethlehem. After Herod was dead, an angel appeared to Joseph again and told him to take the little family back to Israel where they settled in Nazareth. This also fulfilled what had been told by the prophets centuries before—that He would be called a "Nazarene."

Today we would call being from Nazareth living on the wrong side of the tracks or the wrong side of town—not the best schools, not the right clubs, not the best shopping, and certainly no nightlife. But this is where God ordained that His Son be raised in an ordinary family in an ordinary place.

The Future

Jesus lived and worked in this ordinary setting. But His return will be anything but ordinary. Bethlehem is known as the City of David, because it was David's hometown. Samuel came there to anoint him King of Israel as a teenager one thousand years before Christ, pointing to Jesus as the ultimate KING.

The Bible calls Jesus
*   the King of all the earth (Psalm 47:7); and
*   King of kings and Lord of lords (1 Timothy 6:15).

And it tells us that all kings will bow down to him and all nations will serve him (Psalm 72:11).

So we have this truth to look forward to: **Jesus may have been born in a manger—but He is returning as KING.**

In the Meantime

With all this history and fulfilled prophecy, at some point we have to know that Jesus is different. For over two thousand years, He has had a greater impact on people's lives than anyone else in history. He does not make it difficult for us to know Him. He is not stingy with Himself.

We all have some awareness, some knowledge, or some experience with Jesus Christ, even through people around us.

This can be different for everyone.

Maybe you grew up in a Christian home, and faith in Jesus Christ was modeled so beautifully for you that you desired it for yourself, and you're living out your legacy.

Maybe you grew up in a home where God's name was only mentioned as a curse word, in anger, or frustration. And the thought that He is your heavenly Father doesn't sit well with you, because your earthly father was such a bad example. So you want nothing to do with Him.

Or maybe you grew up in a divided home, where one parent believed and followed Jesus, and the other was indifferent or uninterested. You were left in the middle, not knowing which road to take.

But we all grow up, and in His sovereignty God sees to it that we all have some knowledge of Him that tells us He IS different! At the very least, we can just go outside on a clear evening and look up.

The Bible says:

> The heavens declare the glory of God; the skies proclaim the work of his hands. Day after day they pour forth speech; night after night they display knowledge. There is no speech or language where their voice is not heard. Their voice goes out into all the earth, their words to the ends of the world. (Psalm 19:1-4)

The Bible also says that we are without excuse, because God has made Himself known.

> Since the creation of the world God's invisible qualities— his eternal power and divine nature—have been clearly seen, being understood from what has been made, so that men are without excuse. (Romans 1:20)

Yet it's so easy to be blinded to the truth and silence His voice in our noisy world, rather than stopping and listening and responding to Him for ourselves. It's so easy to blend in with the masses. It's so easy to blame our parents or blame our upbringing or blame our circumstances for our negative attitude towards God. Or to use them to rationalize our refusal to simply believe and let Him take over.

At the end of the day and the end of our life, however, we will stand before God alone. He will hold us accountable

- for the knowledge we had or didn't have;
- for the opportunities to know Him that we had—or didn't have;
- for the choices we made—and didn't make; and
- for turning away from Him—instead of to Him.

So it is important we make the connection here.

Jesus came to Bethlehem. Bethlehem means House of Bread. Jesus very fittingly called Himself the Bread of Life meaning when we partake of Him, we live because He is our sustenance and better than any food supplement or vitamin we can take. He feeds us, strengthens us, guides us, comforts us, and energizes us. He gives our life meaning, purpose, satisfaction, fulfillment, and peace. He is the source of everything we need to really live.

You are not alone, traveling through this life with no direction, no compass, and no purpose. Jesus, Immanuel, God with us, was born to show you the way.

Personal Reflection

I grew up in a home where faith wasn't discussed or made to seem important. And if you did have faith, it was best to keep it private. But even as a young child, I sensed God all around me. In fact, I would walk our dog around the corner and tie him to the gate outside a little neighborhood church, which was always open, and go in. I would sit there and soak up the beauty of the dark wood, the stained glass windows, the flickering candles, and the peace that is never present in an alcoholic home. I would leave refreshed and assured that God was there. But He was also with me, and somehow, everything was going to be okay.

And in the end, it will be.

While Waiting His Return

Don't leave Jesus in the manger and don't just bring Him out at Christmas. Let Him rule in your heart and life now, and things will go better for you when you do.

The Bible says:
Blessed are all who fear the Lord, who walk in his ways.
(Psalm 128:1)

This hymn will help us celebrate Christmas every day.

> Hark! the herald angels sing, "Glory to the newborn King!"
> Peace on earth and mercy mild, God and sinners reconciled!
> Joyful all ye nations rise, join the triumph of the skies;
> With th'angelic host proclaim, "Christ is born in Bethlehem!"
> Hark! the herald angels sing, "Glory to the newborn King!"
> ("Hark! The Herald Angels Sing" by Charles Wesley)

Now let's follow Him and learn as we go.

Chapter 3

Presented at the Temple
Returning to Be Worshiped

*J*esus entered the temple in Jerusalem for the first time when He was only eight days old. Mary and Joseph brought Him there to be circumcised. God had given circumcision to the Israelites to distinguish them from the pagan people who occupied the Promised Land before them.

But now, forty days later, they were bringing Him back to dedicate Him to God, also required by Jewish Law. Countless infants had been through the same ceremonies, but Jesus was the only infant who ever came through the gate of this magnificent structure to be greeted as the MESSIAH.

PERHAPS THIS IS WHAT IT LOOKED LIKE
WHEN THEY ENTERED THE TEMPLE

Two important people were there to greet Him. Simeon was an old man who had lived his entire life for God. He was expecting the Messiah, and God honored his heart's desire to see Him before he died. As soon as he saw the young couple with Jesus, he took Him in his arms and prophesied Jesus' divine destiny.

The Bible says **that Simeon said:**
"For my eyes have seen your salvation." (Luke 2:30)

The other person waiting to greet Jesus as the Messiah was a woman, a prophetess and eighty-four-year-old widow named Anna. She too loved God and worshiped in the temple in Jerusalem morning and night, fasting and praying. When she saw Mary and Joseph with the baby Jesus, she knew.

The Bible says:
Coming up to them, she gave thanks to God and spoke about the child to all who were looking forward to the redemption of Jerusalem. (Luke 2:38)

The Promise

The Jewish people were waiting for their long promised Messiah who they hoped would free them from Roman occupation. Little did they know He was coming to save them and us—from so much more. He was coming to redeem us from sin.

Here's the promise: Jesus, the Messiah, came to redeem us from sin, and everyone will worship Him when He returns.

But what does that mean? *The New World Dictionary* defines *redeem* as "to buy back" and *redemption* as "release from sin." It defines *worship* as "honor, dignity, reverence or devotion for a deity" and *worshipful* as "being worthy to be worshiped."

So this child that was anticipated would be a redeemer worthy of worship. Both Simeon and Anna had the privilege of meeting Him that day.

Now we have the privilege of understanding why and how He is to be worshiped.

The Past

Our understanding begins at the temple when Jesus was first recognized as the promised Messiah and coming Redeemer.

The Jewish temple is long gone, but the real estate it occupied is arguably the most contested, coveted, and volatile piece of property in the world. It is the convergence zone of the world's three major religions: Judaism, Islam, and Christianity.

To understand the significance of both the land and the temple, we have to understand the history. When King David conquered the land one thousand years before Christ, it was his desire to build a temple of worship to the One True God of Israel in the midst of the pagan worship around him.

Ever since being freed from bondage under the Egyptian Pharaoh and led through the wilderness to the Promised Land by Moses, the Israelites had worshiped God according to His precise instructions set forth in the books of Exodus, Leviticus, and Deuteronomy. So the animal sacrifices, offerings, priesthood, Feast Days, and laws and regulations around His worship were established.

Initially, this required a portable temple or tabernacle called the Tent of Meeting, which the Israelites could pick up and carry with them on their travels. It housed the Ark of the Covenant containing the Ten Commandments God had given Moses on Mount Sinai, representing God's presence among them. It reminded them of His covenant promise that He was their God, and they were His people.

So now, it was only fitting that David would want to build a more permanent structure of worship for his people. His own words convey that desire.

The Bible says:

> After the king was settled in his palace and the Lord had given him rest from all his enemies around him, he said to Nathan the prophet, "Here I am living in a palace of cedar, while the ark of God remains in a tent." (2 Samuel 7:1-2)

43

The Lord responded to David's desire by reminding him of all He had done for him, bringing him from the Judean desert as a shepherd to this cedar palace in Jerusalem as Israel's king. Then He surprised him by saying, "instead of you building a house for me, I am going to establish a house for you."

The Bible continues:

"When your days are over and you rest with your fathers, I will raise up your offspring to succeed you, who will come from your own body, and I will establish his kingdom. He is the one who will build a house for my Name, and I will establish the throne of his kingdom forever." (2 Samuel 7: 12-13)

In other words, David's legacy would not be a temple of worship for God but a family dynasty through which the promised Messiah would one day come.

In the meantime, David's son Solomon would be the one to actually build the temple in the land David had acquired and on the hill or threshing floor he had purchased to build an altar to the Lord (2 Samuel 24:18).

And so it was that the first temple to the One True God, the God of Abraham, the God of Isaac, and the God of Jacob, whose descendants became the nation of Israel, was constructed.

What a project it was. Solomon, who built the temple in the fourth year of his reign, spared nothing in building it. The exact dimensions are recorded for us in 1 Kings 6, and yet it was unlike any building project of our day.

The Bible says:

In building the temple, only blocks dressed at the quarry were used, and no hammer, chisel or any other tool was heard at the temple site while it was being built. (1 Kings 6:7)

Can you imagine a construction site in Tokyo, Singapore, Seattle, Miami, or Mexico City buzzing with activity and progress and yet not hearing the deafening sounds of heavy machinery, cranes, jack-hammers, and drills?

And can you imagine eighty thousand men assigned to cut the stones at the quarry and seventy thousand men assigned to carry them to the construction site—and thirty-six hundred foremen over-seeing the work so it would be done just as God would have it done (2 Chronicles 2:18). Even the interior workmanship was impeccable with intricate wood carvings, elaborate art work, and gold overlays. The construction of the temple was a sacred time for the Israelites. The reason becomes obvious as Solomon prepared an inner sanctuary overlaid with pure gold and guarded by a pair of carved cherubim to house the Ark of the Covenant, because it symbolized the very pres-ence of God (1 Kings 6:19).

So the days of the Tent of Meeting or traveling tabernacle were over, and the presence of God would now dwell in this magnificent structure dedicated solely to His worship.

We can learn why God is worthy of our worship from excerpts of Solomon's prayer of dedication.

The Bible says:

"O Lord, God of Israel, there is no God like you in heaven above or earth below..." (1 Kings 8:23a)

"But will God really dwell on earth? The heavens, even the highest heaven, cannot contain you. How much less this temple I have built." (1 Kings 8:27)

"May your eyes be open toward this temple night and day, this place of which you said, 'My Name shall be there,' so that you will hear the prayer your servant prays toward this place." (1 Kings 8:29)

"...and when you hear, forgive." (1 Kings 8:30)

The Bible continues:

"May the Lord our God be with us...may he never leave us nor forsake us. May he turn our hearts to him, to walk in all his ways and to keep the commands...he gave our fathers. (1 Kings 8:57-58)

...so that all the peoples of the earth may know that the
Lord is God and that there is no other." (1 Kings 8:60)

According to Scripture, God alone is worthy of our worship. The
Jewish temple built by Solomon with God's help was the appropriate
place to honor and worship Him. But as awe-inspiring as this structure was, it fell to the Babylonians when they conquered Jerusalem
in 586 BC. The temple was stripped of its treasures and burned. The
city walls were destroyed and people were taken and held captive
as slaves in Babylon for seventy years (2 Chronicles 36:15-21). We
can't help but ask why? Why would God allow such a thing?

The answer is found in the leadership of the people. A whole line
of evil kings did evil deeds in the sight of the Lord (2 Chronicles
36). Instead of turning to Him, they turned away and hardened their
hearts toward Him. The prophet Jeremiah warned them and even
prophesied what would happen if they didn't change, but to no avail.

The Bible says:

The Lord, the God of their fathers, sent word to them
through his messengers again and again, because he
had pity on his people and on his dwelling place. But
they mocked God's messengers, despised his words and
scoffed at his prophets until the wrath of the Lord was
aroused against his people and there was no remedy. He
brought up against them the king of the Babylonians...
(2 Chronicles 36:15-17)

And the king of the Babylonians carried them into exile (2
Chronicles 36:20).

As the leader goes, so go the people. Thankfully for the Jewish
people, Persia came to power, and Cyrus, the king, was a God-fearing
man who listened to what the prophet Jeremiah had said and issued
this proclamation.

The Bible says that Cyrus said:

"The Lord, the God of heaven, has given me all the kingdoms of the earth and he has appointed me to build a

temple for him at Jerusalem in Judah. Anyone of his people among you—may his God be with him, and let him go up to Jerusalem in Judah and build the temple of the Lord, the God of Israel, the God who is in Jerusalem." (Ezra 1:2-3)

And so it was that Cyrus helped the exiles return to their beloved city and under the leadership of Ezra and Zerubbabel restored the temple. However, the Ark of the Covenant was never found or replaced.

The temple wasn't totally rebuilt until Herod the Great came to power in 37 BC. Herod wanted to gain the favor of the Jews in his jurisdiction as well as impress his Roman subjects by making the temple bigger and better than it had ever been. He added elaborate porches, gates, arches, and stairways, although the center portion remained on the exact spot, or the threshing floor, that David had purchased so many centuries before.

The central purpose of the temple remained the same: the place of worship to the One True God of Israel. This was the place the people could come to receive forgiveness for their sins. Forgiveness is crucial to worship because sin keeps us from seeing God as God. He is holy and perfect in all His ways. He is the Creator and sustainer of the universe and the sovereign ruler over all creation. Sin is any violation of God's law as set forth in the Ten Commandments. Sin keeps the focus on us. God's forgiveness puts the focus on Him.

The procedure for His forgiveness was always the same. The person would come to the temple with an animal to sacrifice—a dove if they were of little means, a lamb if they could afford it, but both had to be perfect specimens. They would bring their sacrifice to the priest and confess their sins over it, symbolically transferring their sins to it. Then they would kill the animal, and the priest would sprinkle its blood on the altar.

God Himself had prepared the Israelites for this pattern of worship while they were still slaves in Egypt. The Pharaoh had refused to let them leave and return to their land. So after sending many plagues to convince him, God instructed the Israelites, through Moses, to kill a lamb, one for each family, and spread its blood over the doorposts of their home. His final plague to force the Pharaoh's hand would be the angel of death coming through the land to kill all firstborn sons, including the Pharaoh's. The Israelites' homes, with the blood over the door, would be spared. They would literally be passed over.

This established animal sacrifices in the Old Testament as God's method to worship Him. But why kill a poor innocent animal?

The Bible says:

> The life of a creature is in the blood and I have given it to you to make atonement for yourselves on the altar; it is the blood that makes atonement for one's life. (Leviticus 17:11)

> ...without the shedding of blood there is no forgiveness. (Hebrews 9:22)

Something has to die for us to live. God set it up that way. He had the right. He created us. He chose to love us in spite of our sin. He chose to come and die in our place for our sin. He was preparing us to recognize our sinfulness and realize our need for a Savior.

All the animal sacrifices in the Old Testament are designed to point to the one, perfect, and sufficient sacrifice that Jesus Christ would make to atone, or make amends, for the sins of the world in the New Testament. At that point in time, animal sacrifices would no longer be necessary. Their role would be fulfilled in God's plan of redemption for the human race.

Shortly after Jesus' death and resurrection, which ended the need for animal sacrifices to atone for sin, the magnificent temple that Herod built, as more of a tribute to himself than the God he tried to impress and contain, was destroyed in AD 70, when the Roman armies invaded Jerusalem. The only reminder that it ever existed is the Temple Mount, or that same area, the threshing floor that David had purchased when he came to power as King of Israel.

The Future

The centuries reveal man's need to worship, and the future will perfect our understanding that Jesus Christ alone is worthy of our worship. History is moving toward His return when that will be fulfilled. This tiny piece of land will always play a vital role in that process.

Today the temple area is occupied by the Muslims who built the Dome of the Rock as a shrine to their god Mohammed in the seventh century after Christ. It has never been destroyed. The land is important to them because it is where Mohammed had his vision. His footprint is said to be left on the rock, the rock also known as Mount Moriah.

THE DOME OF THE ROCK

The site is equally important to Jews and Christians because Mount Moriah is where Abraham was willing to sacrifice his son, Isaac. Scholars also believe this is where God created Adam and Eve. God's throne is thought to be directly above it, and the location of the inner sanctuary of the Jewish temple, or the Holy of Holies, is thought to be just to the right of the Dome of the Rock. In fact, many orthodox Jews will not even walk there for fear of stepping on this most sacred place.

SITE THOUGHT TO BE THE HOLY OF HOLIES

But the temple area is also where the only remaining section of the walls surrounding the temple exists. For the Jews, the Western Wall, or the Wailing Wall as it is often called, is considered to be their holiest place on earth.

According to the travel brochures, it is also the most visited site in the world by Christians. Day in and day out, people stand in line to press their little pieces of paper, containing a carefully written prayer, into a crevice of this wall. Standing there, one can sense the basic need of the human heart to connect with the God who created us and knows our inner struggles and deepest pain.

Most importantly, however, the temple is where Jesus transitioned our thinking from the idea of a temple made by human hands of rocks and stones to a living temple. Solomon was right when he said God cannot be contained.

After Jesus' death and resurrection, He sent His Holy Spirit to live in the hearts of all who believe, and we become the temple for God to live in.

THIS WRITER AT THE WAILING WALL

The Bible says:

> Don't you know that you yourselves are God's temple
> and that God's Spirit lives in you? ...God's temple is
> sacred and you are that temple. (1 Corinthians 3:16-17)

Believers are the new temple of worship. Each one of us is a
building stone put in place by God Himself to create His church,
the Body of believers around the world. Jesus Christ is the foundation stone or capstone or cornerstone and every believer adds to its
strength and fulfills a unique place just as each stone was perfectly
fitted in Solomon's temple. All of our life's experiences are the quarry
that molds us and shapes us for the role we are to play as part of
God's family.

The Bible continues:

> You are no longer foreigners and aliens, but fellow cit-
> izens with God's people and members of God's house-
> hold, built on the foundation of the apostles and prophets,

with Christ Jesus himself as the chief cornerstone. In him the whole building is joined together and rises to become a holy temple in the Lord. And in him you too are being built together to become a dwelling in which God lives by his Spirit. (Ephesians 2:19-22)

We can worship Jesus now anywhere, anytime, not just in church, because He lives in the hearts of believers. But some day, everyone will worship Him. The truth we need to understand is: **Jesus Christ is returning to be worshiped**.

When He does,

The Bible says:
Every knee will bow, in heaven and on earth and under the earth, and every tongue confess that Jesus Christ is Lord, to the glory of God the Father. (Philippians 2:10-11)

It will no longer be an option to kneel before Jesus and acknowledge Him as LORD. Why not bow before Him now, and save ourselves the embarrassment and the shame of refusing the gift of salvation He came to offer.

The Bible tells us the prophet Isaiah had a vision of Jesus in His heavenly temple that caused him to tremble.

The Bible says:
In the year that King Uzziah died, I saw the Lord seated on a throne, high and exalted, and the train of his robe filled the temple. Above him were seraphs, each with six wings: with two wings they covered their faces, with two they covered their feet, and with two they were flying.

And they were calling to one another: "Holy, holy, holy is the Lord Almighty; the whole earth is full of his glory."

At the sound of their voices the doorposts and thresholds shook and the temple was filled with smoke.

"Woe to me!" I cried. "I am ruined! For I am a man of unclean lips, and I live among a people of unclean lips,

and my eyes have seen the King, the Lord Almighty."
(Isaiah 6:1-5)

Isaiah trembled because he saw what we will all see when Jesus
Christ returns. We will see His majesty, His absolute power, and His
unmistakable GLORY! At that point in time, every knee WILL bow,
and we will worship Him.

In the Meantime

We no longer have to go to a temple, purchase an animal to sacrifice, take it to the priest, confess our sins over it, kill it, and sprinkle
its blood on the altar to receive forgiveness for our sins. Thank God,
Jesus Christ died for us so we don't have to. We no longer have to
wait for a priest to enter the inner sanctuary, or the Holy of Holies, and
make atonement for our sins or for the sins of our nation once a year.

We have direct access to God the Father because Jesus IS the
Messiah. He IS the promised Savior of the world. He chose to leave
heaven and come to this earth as one of us and die for us, so the debt
for our sin is paid. There is no other way to bridge the gap between
ourselves and a holy God. Sin creates the barrier that cannot be
broken, crossed, or torn down and is a debt we cannot pay. There is
no way to escape our fate. The math is easy: 1 sin = debt. We all owe
the debt, because who can say,

- I've never stolen;
- I've never wanted what wasn't mine;
- I've never lusted in my heart;
- I've never neglected God;
- I've never despised His Name?

The Bible issues the verdict: All have sinned and fall short of the
glory of God (Romans 3:23) and "There is no one righteous, not even
one" (Romans 3:10).

God is perfection and anything less separates us from Him. That's
why anything other than His own Son, Himself in human form, would
fail to bridge the gap or pay the price or open the way for us to be
with Him again.

The debt we owe is payable in blood only. A life—a righteous life—had to be taken in order for us to be made right before Him. Jesus provided His righteousness.

The Bible says:

> God made him who had no sin to be sin for us, so that in him we might become the righteousness of God. (2 Corinthians 5:21)

The Bible also says:

> All are justified freely by his grace through the redemption that came by Christ. God presented him as a sacrifice of atonement, through faith in his blood... (Romans 3:24-25)

This is why the blood of Jesus is so very precious. It was shed for you and for me. This is what redemption means. Jesus died so we could be set free. Free to love, free to forgive, free to worship, and free to live the life we are created to live. But He forces Himself on no one.

The choice is ours. We are not puppets that have to respond to God's great love for us. Instead, He created us with a free will to allow us to choose. After all, what kind of relationship is born out of power, force, control, or intimidation? God seeks people who choose to respond to His love with love. Jesus provides the way, the only way (John 14:6). But people always try to come their own way. It's no different now than it was when Jesus came to earth. Like the ancient pagans, we fashion our own gods:

- the god of materialism,
- the god of secularism,
- the god of vanity,
- the god of busyness,
- the god of status and prestige,
- the god of pleasure and leisure,
- the god of SELF—selfish ambition, self-absorption, and self-esteem.

We worship them in place of the One who redeemed us from such short-sighted pursuits.

Why do we worship Jesus?

Jesus alone is worthy of our worship because He is God in the flesh. He lived and died to redeem us from our sin, so we could be reconciled to God. And His resurrection from the dead proves we will be. No wonder He will not share His position with any of the false gods of our own making. He is a *jealous* God (Exodus 20:5), because He loves us. So He draws us to Himself to worship Him now, because time is running out.

How do we worship Jesus?

God created us to have an intimate relationship with Him. Therefore, He desires our hearts over our head knowledge, our obedience over our sacrifices, and our worship over our words. Worship includes knowing His Word to us through the Bible, communicating to Him through prayer, and attending a church that strengthens us in those pursuits. Worship combines an attitude of heart and mind as well as action to back it up.

We worship God the way we live in our thinking, our decision making, our attitudes, our conversations, our relationships, and our priorities. So that the people around us, like the people who heard Solomon's prayer, know that we worship the One True and Only God, the Lord Jesus Christ.

Personal Reflection

My first experience with true worship was through my maternal grandmother. We spent summers with her in Colorado. Because she was a widow and I was the oldest girl of four siblings, I slept with her. I remember waking up in the wee hours of the morning and watching her with one eye open, so she wouldn't see me, as she began her daily routine. First, came the vigorous calisthenics which she would say later "got her circulation going." Then she would kneel by the bed to pray. Her deep reverence and love for God were obvious and compelling. It made an indelible impression on my young mind and initiated a spiritual curiosity that eventually led me to wanting the same relationship with Him. I am forever grateful for that memory and am continually inspired to have the same impact on my own family and beyond.

While Waiting His Return

What should we do?

We should turn to Jesus and worship Him the way He deserves to be worshiped—with heart, mind and spirit—as the One, True, and Only God.

And we should let the world know what we believe and why, so everyone we come in contact with also comes in contact with the Living God.

We are the temple in which He dwells. We are to act like it and invite others in while waiting for Him to return.

Hymns of the faith help us worship God. This one is a great way to begin each day.

Holy, Holy, Holy! Lord God Almighty!
Early in the morning our song shall rise to Thee;
Holy, Holy, Holy! Merciful and Mighty!
God in three Persons, blessed Trinity!
("Holy, Holy, Holy! Lord God Almighty" by Reginald Heber)

Now let's go with Jesus to the River Jordan where He is baptized.

Chapter 4

Baptized in the River Jordan
Returning for His Own

here are two basic questions everyone asks at one time or another: "Why am I here?" and "Where am I going?" As human beings we need to know. We need to know who we are, what our purpose is and why our life matters. It distinguishes us from the animal kingdom and establishes our responsibility and worth. So how we answer those two questions determines how we live, who we become, and how we die. During our life, we are all identified with something: some cause, some belief, some career, some lifestyle, some family, some person.

The Promise

Baptism is the act by which we are identified with God. So before Jesus began His public ministry at the age of thirty, He purposefully sought out His forerunner, John the Baptist, to baptize Him, because He knew His purpose, He knew His calling, and He knew His destiny. He knew His identity was with God.

> **Here's the promise:** We can know the same. We can know our purpose, our calling, and our destiny. We can claim identity with God now, before Jesus returns.

The Past

John was six months Jesus' senior, and God had ordained that he would be His forerunner who would announce His arrival as the Messiah. John was preaching out in the desert of Judea to anyone who would come out to hear him.

So of course there were the curious who just wanted to hear this man rant and rave and who wanted to ridicule his clothes, his diet, and his lifestyle. And there were the seekers, who were looking for the answers to our two questions and hoping John could help them find the answer. And there were the religious leaders, who were wondering if he was the Messiah. All four gospels help us visualize the scene.

From Matthew's gospel, *the Bible says*:

In those days John the Baptist came, preaching in the Desert of Judea and saying, "Repent, for the kingdom of heaven is near." This is he who was spoken by the prophet Isaiah: "A voice of one calling in the desert, 'Prepare the way for the Lord, make straight paths for him.'" (Matthew 3:1-3)

Luke's gospel clarifies the timing. *The Bible says:*

In the fifteenth year of the reign of Tiberius Caesar—when Pontius Pilate was governor of Judea, Herod tetrarch of Galilee, his brother Philip tetrarch of Iturea and Traconitis, and Lysanias tetrarch of Abilene—during the high priesthood of Annas and Caiaphas, the word of God came to John son of Zechariah in the desert. (Luke 3:1-2)

Luke's information is important because it verifies the time, the place, the people, and the events through secular history. So this is not a myth or a legend, but the documented debut of Jesus' public ministry.

From Mark's gospel, *the Bible says:*

And so John came, baptizing in the desert region and preaching a baptism of repentance for the forgiveness of sins. The whole Judean countryside and all the people of Jerusalem went out to him. Confessing their sins, they were baptized by him in the Jordan River. John wore clothing made of camel's hair, with a leather belt around his waist, and he ate locusts and wild honey. And this was his message: "After me will come one more powerful than I, the thongs of whose sandals I am not worthy to stoop down and untie. I baptize you with water, but he will baptize you with the Holy Spirit." (Mark 1:4-8)

This, too, is important, because John the Baptist knows who he is and who he is NOT. So when the religious leaders come out to see what's going on, he tells them.

The Bible says:
Now this was John's testimony when the Jews of Jerusalem sent priests and Levites to ask him who he was. He did not fail to confess, but confessed freely, "I am not the Christ."

They asked him, "Then who are you? Are you Elijah?"

He said, "I am not."

"Are you the Prophet?"

He answered, "No."

Finally they said, "Who are you? Give us an answer to those who sent us. What do you say about yourself? … Why then do you baptize if you are not the Christ, nor Elijah, nor the Prophet?" (John 1:19-22, 25)

In other words, what are your credentials, John? What right do you have to be preaching? Who sent you? And what are we supposed to tell the Governor?

John's gospel continues. *The Bible says:*
The next day John (the Baptist) saw Jesus coming toward him and said, "Look, the Lamb of God, who takes away the sin of the world! This is the one that I meant when I said, 'A man who comes after me has surpassed me

because he was before me.' I myself did not know him, but the reason I came baptizing with water was that he might be revealed to Israel."

Then John gave this testimony: "I saw the Spirit come down from heaven as a dove and remain on him. I would not have known him, except that the one who sent me to baptize with water told me, 'The man on whom you see the Spirit come down and remain is he who will baptize with the Holy Spirit.' I have seen and I testify that this is the Son of God." (John 1:29-34)

An astounding statement that changed the world forever!

John the Baptist is telling the world that Jesus is God's remedy for the sins of mankind. As God's ultimate provision to rescue people out of sin and into fellowship with Himself, He is the perfect, unblemished substitute God had required in the Old Testament, appearing in the New. John is saying that Jesus is the eternal God in the flesh. He was in the beginning, God, and in the end, God. He was revealing Himself to Israel and then to the world through Israel. John would not have known that Jesus was the Son of God unless God Himself had told him, because God in the flesh was so ordinary, so non-spectacular, so one of us, that He blended in with us. So God gave John the ultimate clue. The One on whom My Spirit rests is HIM. He is the Messiah.

Before that day, John had just done his job and waited. Every day more people came to hear him preach, because people then were just as desperate as people today. They wanted answers, they wanted hope, they wanted release from their stress and fears. They wanted peace of mind and spirit.

Then one day, Jesus came. And we know that John knew who He was because, after all, they were cousins. They grew up in the same area. They were family. But Jesus wasn't a show-off or a braggart. He didn't go around flaunting His title or wearing a badge saying, "I am the Messiah." Therefore, when Jesus appeared at the River Jordan to be baptized, and the Spirit of God hovered over Him, and a thundering voice from heaven announced, "This is my Son, whom I love; with him I am well pleased" (Matthew 3:17), there was no mistaking Jesus' identity. John knew it, accepted it, submitted to it—and baptized Jesus. And from that day forward, John said, "He must become greater; I must become less" (John 3:30).

BAPTISMAL SITE AT THE RIVER JORDAN

John had done his job well. So well that people heard and responded to the message. The same message we need to hear today: repent, turn around, do a complete 180, and turn back to God. Repentance means change. Change your mind, change your attitude, change your focus, change your priorities, change your direction. Push the reset button, and let God change your life. Live for God instead of yourself. Make Him #1, and your life will take on new meaning and new purpose, and you will find fulfillment in the process.

But everyone responds differently to the same message. While many were recognizing their need and making a public declaration of their repentance, the religious leaders, who should have recognized the signs and remembered the Old Testament prophecies and welcomed Jesus as their Messiah, resisted Him. John knew the Scriptures, saw right through their hypocrisy, and addressed it.

The Bible says:

> When he saw many of the Pharisees and Sadducees coming to where he was baptizing, he said to them: "You brood of vipers! Who warned you to flee from the coming wrath? Produce fruit in keeping with repentance. And do not think you can say to yourselves, 'We have Abraham as our father.' I tell you that out of these stones God can raise up children for Abraham." (Matthew 3:7-9)

And then John the Baptist adds:

> "After me will come one who is more powerful than I, ... His winnowing fork is in his hand, and he will clear his threshing floor, gathering his wheat into the barn and burning up the chaff with unquenchable fire." (Matthew 3:11-12)

These were harsh words no one likes to hear. The truth can hurt, but even so, John knew how important it was and he wasn't afraid to speak it. He was not intimidated by his audience. His confidence was not in himself but in God and His revealed Word. So he didn't pander to the religious leaders from Jerusalem. And he didn't water down his message for fear of offending them. He knew they were resting on their religion and their Jewish roots in Abraham, much like we may assume that just because we were baptized as a baby, or confirmed as a teenager, and have the documents in a drawer to prove it, that we are in good standing with God.

But John shatters their thinking and ours by pointing to the fruit. Where's the fruit? In other words, how does your life line up with what you say you believe? The religious leaders followed the Old Testament Law to the letter and even added hundreds more, to make doubly sure they would impress God. It became tedious to be a Jew, to the point where you couldn't tie your shoe on the Sabbath or carry anything weighing more than a fig!

John cuts right through their hypocrisy, their stubbornness, and their self-righteousness. He tells his audience: "The proof of their relationship with God is in repentance because only repentance leads to a changed life. And only a changed life produces fruit for God" (Matthew 3:8-10).

So John wasted no opportunity in trying to correct wrong thinking and warn of impending disaster for refusing to change. His reference to the threshing floor refers back to the temple foundation where the sacrifices were made in the Old Testament and basically says: God knows your heart. God sees your motives and your intent. God knows why you're here and what you're looking for. God recognizes a fake when He sees it. And now He's warning you. When He comes again, He'll separate the true believers from the pretenders.

John's ministry came to an abrupt end while in prison for confronting Herod about his adulterous relationship with his brother's wife. He died a despicable death. No one deserves to have their head chopped off and delivered to a party on a platter (Matthew 14:8-11). But today John continues to enjoy an indescribable eternity, because he obeyed God, knew his calling, taught the truth, and stayed true to the end.

The Bible says:

It has now been revealed through the appearing of our Savior, Christ Jesus, who has destroyed death and has brought life and immortality to light through the gospel. (2 Timothy 1:10)

The Future

This same life and immortality await us when we put our faith in Jesus because the truth is: **Jesus is returning for His own.**

Then we will understand the importance of the River Jordan. It represents all the blessings God has in store for believers. It symbolizes the cleansing that takes place when we repent of our sin and come to Christ for salvation.

The Bible says:

> There is a river whose streams make glad the city of God,
> the holy place where the Most High dwells. (Psalm 46:4)

The Apostle John had this vision:

> Then the angel showed me the river of the water of life,
> as clear as crystal, flowing from the throne of God and of
> the Lamb down the middle of the great street of the city.
> On each side of the river stood the tree of life, bearing
> twelve crops of fruit, yielding its fruit every month. And
> the leaves of the tree are for the healing of the nations.
> No longer will there be any curse. The throne of God
> and of the Lamb will be in the city, and his servants will
> serve him. They will see his face, and his name will be
> on their foreheads. There will be no more night. They
> will not need the light of a lamp or the light of the sun, for
> the Lord God will give them light. And they will reign
> forever and ever. (Revelation 22:1-5)

This is heaven come down to earth and it is written right before
Jesus says: "Behold, I am coming soon" (Revelation 22:7).

In the Meantime

The River Jordan held importance in the past for the nation of
Israel, it holds importance in the future when Jesus returns, and it
holds importance for us in the present because it points out our need
for repentance—symbolized by baptism.

That's why we need to understand baptism. Not the ceremony of
baptism and the false sense of security it can give us, but the significance of baptism from the standpoint of repentance.

So why did Jesus choose to be baptized when we know He had
nothing to repent? (2 Corinthians 5:21)

Jesus chose to be baptized to show us our need to repent and to
lead us to Him. Water has always been known as a cleansing agent,
but it can only clean the outside, not the inside. So when the people
came to John and were willing to admit they were sinners in need

of cleansing, he knew they were ready to meet the One who could change them on the inside.

The River Jordan provided the perfect place. It's the strategic river in Israel. It runs north and south, from the three tributaries that feed into the Sea of Galilee in the north, down to the Dead Sea in the south. It was accessible to everyone. It had a significant history with the Jewish people, most notably following the Exodus when they crossed it to enter the Promised Land (Joshua 3:15-17).

THE RIVER JORDAN

The River Jordan draws us in and teaches us that we must come to God His way. It points us to the cross where the transaction is made. We're all given a limited time to get over ourselves and understand our need for His Son, Jesus Christ. It's an individual transaction. No one gets to heaven on the coattails of his parents, or on his pastor's recommendation, or his generous donations, or his record of achievements or good reputation, or his charm and good looks, or his baptismal certificate in his drawer. And we can baptize or dedicate our babies at birth, but those babies must grow up and choose for themselves as well.

Everyone will stand before God on his own and have to pass His test. And He has given us every opportunity and a lifetime to pass it, because there's only one question: "What did you do with my Son?"

So you see, we must answer those two questions we all ask of ourselves sooner or later—"Why am I here?" and "Where am I going?"—because our answer determines our destiny.

Am I a child of God; is my identity with Him? Or am I still resisting Him and trying to make my own way through life?

Do I know where I'm going in this life and after?

We can visit lots of places while we're alive and take many wonderful trips, but there are only two final destinations, and we will end up at one or the other. Heaven is reserved for those who have chosen to come to God His way, the way of repentance, the way of seeing ourselves the way He sees us. We are sinners in desperate need of His Son. Jesus took the punishment that we deserve because of our sin and died in our place. Accepting His sacrifice on our behalf permits us to stand before a holy God, based on Jesus' righteousness alone. Hell is reserved for those who refuse this offer.

God has told us very clearly how we can be among His number:

- it is not a secret club;
- it is not about rituals and traditions;
- it is not about following certain laws;
- it is not even about going to church every week.

It is about saying "YES" to Jesus and letting Him be Lord in our lives.

When we do, His Holy Spirit moves in and takes over, and we are born again. We come to life—spiritually. That new birth points our life in a new direction. From then on, we want to please God, obey God, serve God, and worship God, because God Himself is living in us.

At that point, our reservation is made in heaven under the Name of Jesus Christ with His personal guarantee for all eternity. Then water baptism takes its rightful place and becomes the outward symbol for what has taken place in our hearts.

Is your reservation made? If not, now is a good time to bow your heart to Almighty God and pray this life-changing prayer:

Dear Lord Jesus,

Thank you for revealing this truth to me. I accept your offer of salvation. Please forgive my sins. Come into my life and help me to live for you from here on out. Amen

This is what we were created for. This is who we are and why we're here, because Jesus wants our company in heaven.

The Bible says:
> So Christ was sacrificed once to take away the sins of many people; and he will appear a second time, not to bear sin, but to bring salvation to those who are waiting for him. (Hebrews 9:28)

Personal Reflection

My brother passed away after a ten-year battle with multiple myeloma. He was a strong believer. He lived for God. When he took his last breath, after being in a coma for several days surrounded by family and friends singing his favorite hymns, a smile came across his face, and his last remaining sibling to become a believer believed.

Whether we experience death or are the generation that will see no death but are caught up to meet the Lord in the air, in the great event called the Rapture, we will immediately be with Jesus. And we'll spend eternity thanking Him.

While Waiting His Return

What can we do but praise God?
Praise Him for pursuing you.
Praise Him for His gift of salvation that brings you eternal life—now.
And ask Him what He wants you to do for Him until He returns.

This hymn will put a smile on your face.

Join all the glorious names of wisdom, love, and power,
That ever mortals knew that angels ever bore;
All are too mean to speak His worth, too mean to set my Savior forth.

Great prophet of my God, my tongue would bless Thy Name;
By Thee the joyful news of our salvation came;
The joyful news of sins forgiven, of hell subdued, and peace
    with heaven.
("Join All the Glorious Names" by Isaac Watts)

Now let's follow Jesus out to the Judean desert.

Chapter 5

Tempted in the Wilderness
Returning as Final Victor

*C*ertainly one downside of living in the twenty-first century with all the information and technology we enjoy is the temptation to ignore the One who endowed us with the curiosity, creativity, and the ability to make it all happen.

Jesus knew all about temptation.

The Bible says:

> Then Jesus was led by the Spirit into the desert to be tempted by the devil. After fasting forty days and forty nights, he was hungry. The tempter came to him and said, "If you are the Son of God, tell these stones to become bread." (Matthew 4:1-3)

THE JUDEAN WILDERNESS TODAY

The Promise

We don't have to stay stuck in temptation or the self-destructive behavior it can produce when we give in to its power. Jesus overcame the devil in the wilderness, defeated him on the cross, and proved victory over sin with His resurrection from the dead. His victory then gives us victory now.

> **Here's the promise:** Jesus is returning to prove His final victory over the devil and the evil he represents.

The Past

To understand who this devil is and how he works, let's go to the Judean desert where he tempted Jesus.

Both Mark and Luke add that this was immediately after Jesus' baptism in the Jordan River (Mark 1:12; Luke 4:1). So the timing is interesting, but so is the place. And why would God lead Jesus out there only to come face-to-face with the devil himself?

Jesus had just made His public debut. He had received God's blessing and everyone heard it. He hadn't even begun His ministry. But instead of moving into the spotlight, He is sent out to the Judean wilderness alone, with no snacks, sleeping bag, or even a water bottle.

Why?

Addressing that question helps us understand the battle that people have faced since Adam and Eve succumbed to temptation in the Garden of Eden. God had placed them in a beautiful place with everything they needed. And they were perfectly content, until the devil came along and made them question everything they had and everything God had said. The rest is history. They listened to his lies, succumbed to the temptation, and disobeyed God. At that point in time, we could say, the devil won.

But who is this devil? The Bible identifies him as Satan, the father of lies, Lucifer, the great deceiver, the destroyer, the accuser, the prince or ruler of this world, and the god of this age. He had been an angel in heaven—not just any angel, but an archangel with exquisite beauty. But he wasn't content either.

In fact, he wanted to be God.

So one day there was a war in heaven, and God sent him plummeting to earth, and he's had the run of it ever since (Revelation 12:7-9; Isaiah 14:12-14).

That is, until Jesus came to win us back to God.

Satan wasted no time in confronting the human Jesus, just as he had Adam and Eve in the Garden. He knew Jesus had set aside His divine nature and taken on our human nature. So naturally, Jesus was hungry and hot and tired and susceptible, and could have easily been caught off guard. Satan tempted Him to take the easy way out—to take care of Himself and give in to His humanity. So he tempted Jesus in three distinct ways, hoping at least one would make Him give in.

First, Satan tempted Jesus with food.

Who wouldn't be hungry after spending forty days and nights in the desert, or anywhere for that matter? But Jesus had purposely been fasting, so we know He was also praying. This was part of His preparation for His public ministry that was about to begin. He knew what was ahead. He knew the opposition He would face. He knew the suffering He would endure. But in His mind, we were worth it. So He prepared Himself by removing Himself from every other distraction and spending time alone with God in prayer.

Then Satan came. Seemingly out of nowhere. And looking at the numerous stones that mark the Judean desert, he told Jesus to simply use His divine power to change one of them into bread, and the terrible hunger that was gripping Him would be satisfied.

A CLOSER LOOK AT THE STONES—THEY EVEN LOOK LIKE BREAD

But because Jesus was filled up with God, and because His focus was on God instead of on His own hunger, He could respond with God's Word.

The Bible says Jesus said:

"It is written: 'Man does not live on bread alone, but on every word that comes from the mouth of God.'" (Matthew 4:4)

It wasn't that Jesus didn't love to eat. The Bible makes a point of telling us that He went to a wedding feast in Cana and cooked fish for His disciples on the beach (John 2:1-2; John 21:9-13). It also tells us about a grand feast that all believers will attend in heaven, called the Wedding Supper of the Lamb (Revelation 19:9). The food will be the finest any of us have ever eaten on earth, and the wine will be far superior to the greatest vintage we can buy.

God gave us a great gift in food, because it brings us so much pleasure. It keeps our bodies functioning, our minds sharp, our days organized, and our families together. Satan was very strategic in this temptation, because food is basic to our physical survival. Without it, we die.

But Satan also knew that our most critical need is God.

So his second temptation was to make Jesus doubt God. He took Him to the top of the temple in Jerusalem and quoted God's Word to see if He *really* trusted God.

The Bible says Satan replied:

"If you are the Son of God ... throw yourself down. For it is written: 'He will command His angels concerning you, and they will lift you up in their hands, so that you will not strike your foot against a stone.'" (Matthew 4:6)

In other words, let's see what God will do. Or what all those angels can do to protect you, or if God will even send them.

Jesus wasted no time telling him that God is God and does not need to prove Himself.

The Bible says Jesus said:
> "It is also written: 'Do not put the Lord your God to the test.'" (Matthew 4:7)

Satan didn't have an answer to this, nor did he acknowledge Jesus saying that God is his God too.

Satan was desperate to bring Jesus down. So the third tactic he used to tempt Him was to take Him to a high mountain and show Him all the kingdoms of the world and their splendor, and then say: "All this I will give you if you will bow down and worship me" (Matthew 4:9).

At this point in time, the world was Satan's domain and it still is. Jesus could have succumbed to this temptation and had it all.

But Jesus was prepared to withstand all the temptations Satan could throw at Him. His response to the last was the same as His response to the first. Basically, get lost!!

The Bible says:
> Jesus said to him, "Away from me, Satan! For it is written: 'Worship the Lord your God and serve him only.'" (Matthew 4:10)

Jesus knew what was at stake here. If He gave in, we would have no way back to God. We would have no right to ever stand before Him, no hope of ever seeing His holy heaven, no Savior to save us, and no Redeemer to buy us back from Satan's world, the world of sin, that has condemned us and destined us to hell. That's why God's Spirit led Jesus into the desert. That's why He obeyed. Jesus could have called on all the powers of heaven, but He faced the temptations equipped only with what we, too, have at our disposal—God's Word.

When Satan realized he wasn't going to succeed in tempting Jesus to sin,

The Bible says:
> "The devil left him, and angels came and attended him." (Matthew 4:11)

Luke adds that Satan left him until an opportune time (Luke 4:13). Meanwhile, Jesus was prepared to start His earthly ministry. So He returned to Nazareth and, on the Sabbath, entered the synagogue and began to read from the scroll of the Old Testament prophet Isaiah.

RUINS OF A SYNAGOGUE FROM JESUS' DAY

The Bible says Jesus read:

"The Spirit of the Lord is on me, because he has anointed me to preach good news to the poor. He has sent me to proclaim freedom for the prisoners and recovery of sight for the blind, to release the oppressed, to proclaim the year of the Lord's favor." (Luke 4:18-19 [Isaiah 61:1-2])

After rolling up the scroll and giving it back to the attendant,

The Bible says Jesus said:

"Today this scripture is fulfilled in your hearing." (Luke 4:21)

Jesus was proclaiming to the world for every generation to hear that He was the promised Savior. As such, He was announcing His victory over Satan then. And His dominance over him in the future.

The Future

The Book of Revelation tells us that Satan will have a dismal end.

The Bible says:

> And the devil, who deceived them, was thrown into the lake of burning sulfur...and will be tormented day and night forever and ever. (Revelation 20:10)

Jesus conquers Satan once and for all.

So the truth we have to look forward to is: **Jesus is returning as the final Victor.** He is Victor over sin, over death, and over the devil and we will spend eternity thanking Him for it.

PRESENT DAY MARKER OF JESUS'
VICTORY IN THE JUDEAN WILDERNESS

In the Meantime

Satan is still alive and well on planet Earth. He is the source of all the evil we experience. We live with it every day and experience it in a variety of ways. He will always tempt us the way he tempted

Jesus—through our physical or perceived needs, through our perception of God, and through our pride. If he can't get us one way, he'll try another, because we are vulnerable in all these areas. We are vulnerable to feeling deprived, unnoticed or forgotten by God, and unimportant to everyone else.

Jesus went into the wilderness to show us the way out of any wilderness we find ourselves in. It's the way of strength, not weakness. It's having confidence in God and not giving in to self-pity. It is knowing, believing, and trusting His Word, so we don't believe Satan's lies.

God led Jesus into the wilderness, and He subjected Himself to Satan's temptations to encourage us, because we will all have wilderness experiences. At some point in our lives, we might find ourselves in

- the wilderness of pain and suffering;
- the wilderness of chronic disease;
- the wilderness of loneliness or despair;
- the wilderness of fear or rejection;
- the wilderness of addiction or abuse;
- the wilderness of broken relationships;
- the wilderness of hurtful memories; or
- the wilderness of a broken heart.

We will never face such brutal testing in such brutal conditions as Jesus did. He faced them for us, and He overcame them for us. He showed us the way. His victory in the wilderness teaches us some valuable lessons:

- Satan is strong but God is stronger.
- Satan is a powerful enemy but he is a defeated foe.
- Satan tempts us to sin, but God gives us the strength to resist.
- Temptation is not sin; succumbing to temptation is.
- Our wilderness experiences are allowed by God to draw us closer to Him.
- God establishes the boundaries and is there with us.
- We have victory over Satan only through Jesus.
- God honors our faith and faithfulness.

Yet just like Satan tried to do with Jesus, he strives to plant doubt in our minds. He strives to make us question God's goodness, His power, His provision, His love, His sovereignty, His forgiveness, and our salvation.

If he can get our focus off God, he is succeeding. We begin to wonder if God even exists. The doubts creep in, and we hear Satan whispering in our ear, "If there really is a God, if He really cared, if He really loves you, if He has so much power, if you have enough faith—things would be different."

The implication is God will heal you or save your marriage or protect your job or give you that promotion.

And when these things don't materialize, Satan tempts us to discount God. We discount God when we

- give up on His methods and timing;
- try to control our circumstances;
- lack gratitude and are discontent;
- think we are above reproach; and
- refuse to forgive.

The problem is when we discount God, we are actually defying God. Satan also tempts us to defy God. We defy God when we

- deny Him His rightful place;
- refuse to acknowledge His authority and power;
- insist on living by our rules instead of His;
- "test the limits" in our behavior and at some level expect Him to take care of us; and
- put ourselves ahead of Him.

The irony is when things go wrong, we always seem to blame God.

After all, who else can we blame for all the terrible things that happen? It's just easiest to blame God. We tend to blame Him for everything: personal problems, family breakups, economic hardship, government chaos, increased violence, natural disasters, world hunger. You name it. Everything that goes wrong is God's fault. We hear it all the time.

The relentless question is always the same: how can God let that happen? When in reality, we live in a sin-filled and Satan-controlled world. Satan is the architect of evil. He works night and day to implement it and has zillions of demons to help him.

How do we fight such a powerful enemy?

The first weapon is God's Word. If we don't know what the Bible says, we will succumb to the world view that denies the power of God, and we will have no defense against Satan. But if we study the Bible for ourselves, we can understand what we're up against and personally experience God's power in our lives.

The second weapon for fighting Satan is to understand sin, because sin is his tool to perpetuate the evil that exists and the harm it produces. Sin is any thought, word, or deed that goes against God. People don't understand sin today. We don't like to hear that we are sinners. So we change the terminology and say, "I blew it," "I goofed," or "I made a mistake." Then we justify it and say, "It could have been worse," "Everyone's doing it," or "This is a different day," and we blame it on twenty-first-century living.

But the definition of sin has not changed. And we hear the inevitable questions:

- Why is there so much evil in the world?
- Why is there so much pain and suffering?
- Why is crime and violence increasing?
- And what's happening in our families and our schools and our government and even in our churches?

The answer to these questions is one little word—sin. And we know that Satan is behind every sin that was ever committed. And he is out to destroy us.

So the third weapon for fighting Satan is to recognize him as the enemy. Yet, many people either think he is a farce or they underestimate his power. We hear comments like, "If I'm going to hell anyway, I might as well have fun in the meantime" or "at least I'll be with all my friends!" But Satan is not a myth or a character to be joked about or taken lightly. He is always on the prowl looking for someone to devour (1 Peter 5:8).

But while it is a mistake to underestimate Satan's power, it is also a mistake to overestimate his power. No power above the earth, on the earth, or below the earth can match the power of Almighty God.

And He does not leave us defenseless against the power of Satan. The Bible explains how God equips us to fight. He supplies us with the resources we need—truth, righteousness, peace, faith, salvation, the Holy Spirit, the Word of God, and prayer (Ephesians 6:13-18). With these resources, we are armed and *ready* to fight.

Satan has not changed his M.O. since the Garden of Eden. He was successful then and he is successful now. He will tempt us at our weakest point. He tempts us to doubt, be afraid, lie, cheat, and gossip. He tempts us to neglect God, put ourselves first, feel superior, entitled, and put upon. He tempts us to be judgmental, self-righteous, arrogant, boastful, and proud. Satan also tempts us to be bitter, resentful, unforgiving, or lacking in respect, gratitude, and love.

Every day is a new day to claim the victory that Jesus provides for us. But we have to hear His voice over Satan's voice, and we have to desire His company over Satan's company, and we must choose salvation from sin over bondage to sin.

So it is important we realize that God's Word on sin has not changed, and the consequences for sin have not changed. But neither has God's provision for sin changed. That provision is JESUS, because He did not succumb to Satan's temptations in the Judean desert.

Personal Reflection

We will always have spiritual battles. Jesus passed the test of His temptation with flying colors, and so can we—with His help.

Several years before my conversion, I was locked in my own spiritual battle. I was young and strong and doing just fine without God, yet deep in my soul I knew He was there—loving me even in my rejection of Him. I remember the inner conflict:

- Should I ignore Him?
- Should I pretend He isn't there?
- Should I busy myself with other pursuits?

About this time, a young pastor from a local church was reaching out to new people in the community. I knew of him because a neighbor had invited me to his church. Now I was watching him from an upstairs window get out of his car and come to my door. He looked nice enough. But I carefully moved away from the window so he wouldn't see me. When I heard the doorbell ring, I simply ignored it and waited for him to leave.

I have often wondered how much grief I would have saved myself, if I had simply opened the door and given God the opportunity to free me from that turmoil.

Thankfully, the day came when I knew I had to choose. Did I want this battle to continue to control my life? Did I really want to be so determined to choose my own course? Or did I want to be free of it and give God the chance to prove Himself?

I made my choice that day, but it took a couple more years and that serious illness I mentioned in chapter 1 before I completely surrendered my life to Jesus Christ.

There isn't a day that goes by that I have not thanked Him for pursuing me, even when I did not want to be pursued, and giving me the same victory He won for us in the wilderness.

While Waiting His Return

It is comforting to know that we don't have to be bogged down by all the uncertainty, insecurity, delusion, confusion, and fear that is permeating our society. Jesus equips us to have victory over Satan's attempts to divert our attention from the One we need to pay attention to.

Where do you need His victory today?

What habit, attitude, emotion, misconception, false teaching, bad memory, or painful experience is draining you and distracting you from realizing God's presence and power in your life?

Are you willing to surrender it to Him so He can free you from its destructive grip?

This hymn will strengthen you for whatever you are facing.

> A Mighty Fortress is our God, a bulwark never failing;
> Our helper He amid the flood of mortal ills prevailing.
> For still our ancient foe doth seek to work us woe;
> His craft and power are great, and armed with cruel hate,
> On earth is not his equal.
>
> Did we in our own strength confide our striving would be losing;
> Were not the right man on our side, the man of God's own choosing.
> Dost ask who that might be? Christ Jesus, it is He;
> Lord Sabaoth, His name, from age to age the same,
> And He must win the battle.
>
> ("A Mighty Fortress is Our God" by Martin Luther)

Now let's follow Jesus to Galilee where He began His public ministry.

Chapter 6

Preaching in Galilee
Returning to Establish His
Kingdom on Earth

*I*t's fun to imagine what it must have been like for the first followers of Jesus the day He entered their lives. The setting was Galilee.

The Old Testament prophet Isaiah had prophesied the scene centuries before; now it was here. Nothing would ever be the same again.

The Bible says:

> When Jesus heard that John had been put in prison he returned to Galilee. Leaving Nazareth, he went and lived in Capernaum, which was by the lake in the area of Zebulun and Naphtali—to fulfill what was said through the prophet Isaiah: "Land of Zebulun and land of Naphtali, the way to the sea, along the Jordan, Galilee of the Gentiles—the people living in darkness have seen a great light; on those living in the land of the shadow of death a light has dawned."
>
> From that time on Jesus began to preach, "Repent, for the kingdom of heaven is near." (Matthew 4:12-17)

The Promise

Galilee became the primary scene of Jesus' ministry. It is located in the northern section of Israel and is well-known for the Sea of Galilee where Jesus called His first disciples.

THE SEA OF GALILEE TODAY

Jesus was walking along the lake's shore one day when He encountered two men casting their nets into the lake.

Simon, also called Peter, and his brother Andrew had no idea when they woke up that morning that this was the day that would change their lives forever. They were just beginning another day's work as fishermen when suddenly Jesus came to them.

The Bible says **Jesus said:**
"Come, follow me, and I will make you fishers of men." (Matthew 4:19)

Here's the promise: Jesus came to introduce His kingdom, and He is returning to establish His kingdom on earth.

The Past

What do you think Peter and Andrew thought? Did fishing for men sound easier than fishing for fish?

Little did they know they were about to be part of the biggest rescue mission in history. And ten more would have the same encounter: two more brothers, James and John, sons of Zebedee; Philip and Bartholomew; Thomas and Matthew; James, son of Alphaeus, and Thaddaeus; Simon called the Zealot and the infamous Judas Iscariot (Matthew 10:2-4).

All were Jews and most were fishermen by trade except for Matthew. As a tax collector for the Romans, he was despised, thought of as a traitor among his own people because he got a kickback.

But all were just ordinary and mostly uneducated, hardworking, everyday people going about their ordinary lives, until Jesus walked into their lives and invited them to be part of His kingdom. Simon and Andrew dropped their nets, James and John left their father, and Matthew abandoned his lucrative tax booth.

The moment Jesus called them, they followed. We're left wondering, what was it about Jesus that made them act so decisively, so impulsively, and what did they tell their families? It must have been very exciting, a whirlwind of activity.

The Bible says:

> Jesus went throughout Galilee, teaching in their synagogues, preaching the good news of the kingdom, and healing every disease and sickness among the people. News about him spread all over Syria, and people brought to him all who were ill with various diseases, those suffering severe pain, the demon-possessed, those having seizures, and the paralyzed, and he healed them. Large crowds from Galilee, the Decapolis, Jerusalem, Judea, and the region across the Jordan followed him. (Matthew 4:23-25)

With no cell phones, texting, email, or tweeting, how did word travel so fast? And how did all these people travel such distances through desert and hill country transporting such sick and incapacitated people? But come they did, and they weren't disappointed. Jesus burst on the scene and made a powerful impact. His authority and power, His wisdom and knowledge, His care and compassion were the "Breaking News" of the day. So everywhere He went, His reputation preceded Him, and the numbers grew.

The four gospel accounts of His life fill us in with the details of His world-changing ministry. His teachings offered a stark contrast to the popular teachings of any age.

His Sermon on the Mount, overlooking the beautiful Sea of Galilee, set the stage.

THE "STADIUM" ON THE SEA OF GALILEE TODAY

The hillside had a natural stadium-like indentation that provided abundant seating and perfect acoustics, so everyone could hear.

From that location, *the Bible says* **Jesus said:**
> "Blessed are the poor in spirit, for theirs is the kingdom of heaven.
> Blessed are those who mourn, for they will be comforted.
> Blessed are the meek, for they will inherit the earth.
> Blessed are those who hunger and thirst for righteousness, for they will be filled.
> Blessed are the merciful, for they will be shown mercy.
> Blessed are the pure in heart, for they will see God.
> Blessed are the peacemakers, for they will be called sons of God.
> Blessed are those who are persecuted because of righteousness, for theirs is the kingdom of heaven.

Blessed are you when people insult you, persecute you and falsely say all kinds of evil against you because of me.

Rejoice and be glad, because great is your reward in heaven, for in the same way they persecuted the prophets who were before you." (Matthew 5:3-12)

Jesus' teaching was and is a culture shock in any generation. It goes against the grain of our sinful nature. It is completely contrary to our logic and understanding of survival and success.

But the people came; the stadium was packed. There were no empty seats. They were hungry to hear more.

So they heard about being salt and light in a world that has lost its flavor and its way. The comparisons still hold true. Food is flavorless without salt, and we can't find our way without light. Jesus provides both through the believers of every generation.

The people also learned the damage of behavior we tolerate today: out of control anger, dishonesty, adultery, casual and convenient divorce. And they heard about basic behavior we should aspire to: loving the unlovable, caring for the poor, generosity, and genuine versus robotic prayer.

And always, Jesus' teaching turns our thinking right side up.

- Are we qualified to judge?
- Are we prepared to be judged by the same standard we use with others?
- Will worry really get us anywhere?
- Did it do us any good to stock up for Y2K?
- Would you really build your house on sand?
- Do people care if you spend hours in church or days without food?
- Does that make them want to follow Jesus?
- If "everyone's doing it," should we?
- If you were God, would you like to hear your own prayers? (Matthew 5-7)

While Jesus' teaching began to annoy and infuriate and threaten the religious leaders, it was like a magnet to the people. They were desperate to hear that there had to be a better way: a better way to think, a better way to behave, a better way to treat each other, a better way to live, a better way to reach God.

Jesus didn't waste any time or any opportunity to shift their focus.

He taught them how to pray with honor and respect to their Creator and Father, a prayer many of us memorized as children. It is complete in reverence for God and recognition of our needs.

***The Bible says* Jesus prayed:**
"Our Father which art in heaven,
Hallowed be Thy name,
Thy kingdom come, Thy will be done
in earth as it is in heaven.
Give us this day our daily bread.
And forgive us our debts, as we forgive our debtors.
And lead us not into temptation, but deliver us from evil:
For thine is the kingdom, and the power,
and the glory, forever. Amen."
(Matthew 6:9-13 [KJV])

And everywhere Jesus went, He healed, He helped, and He challenged. People plagued with demons were freed. Paralytics walked. The blind suddenly saw the light of day for the first time. Water was changed to wine at a party to save the embarrassed host. A little girl was raised from the dead. Sin was exposed. Hypocrisy was condemned. Satan was identified.

Jesus was making it clear there are two paths to take in life. One path leads to Him; the other path leads away from Him. His followers became part of His family then, and they still do (Matthew 7-10; John 2:1-11).

But while Jesus was preaching, His forerunner, John the Baptist, was wasting away in prison, condemned for confronting Herod. He must have been wondering what was happening. Was Jesus proving to really be the Messiah?

John finally had the opportunity to find out, so he sent some of his own disciples to ask Jesus if He was the One they were expecting. Or should they expect someone else?

The Bible says **Jesus replied:**

> "Go back and report to John what you hear and see: The blind receive sight, the lame walk, those who have leprosy are cured, the deaf hear, the dead are raised, and the good news is preached to the poor. Blessed is the man who does not fall away because of me." (Matthew 11:4-6)

Isolation, deprivation, disappointment, frustration can stir up doubts. We don't know how long John was in prison, but after having the privilege of baptizing Jesus and hearing the voice of God confirm His identity, he was removed from the scene. How disappointed he must have been not to follow Jesus himself, not to be included in the Messiah's ministry, to be cast aside and forgotten in the palace dungeon. Yet, Jesus paid him the highest honor.

The Bible says **Jesus said about John:**

> "Among those born of women there has not risen anyone greater than John the Baptist;..." (Matthew 11:11)

Jesus goes on to say that since John had prepared the way for His arrival and introduced Him as the "Lamb of God who would take away the sin of the world," the kingdom of God had come down to earth. All the prophets of the Old Testament spoke of this (Matthew 11:13). Now it was here.

With every passing day and every amazing miracle performed in their midst, the religious leaders became more and more incensed. This was not making them look good. After all, they were the ones God had designated to be the spiritual leaders of the Jewish people. Jesus was upstaging them. The crowds were wild over Him. They followed Him everywhere.

Jesus' earthly ministry was limited to three years. His disciples would take over after He left them. He didn't waste a minute training them for the task.

Feeding five thousand hungry men, and who knows how many women and children, provided a perfect teaching moment. Never mind that He had just received word that John the Baptist had been killed. And never mind His own desire to grieve John's death.

The Bible says:

> When Jesus heard what had happened, he withdrew by boat privately to a solitary place. Hearing of this, the crowds followed him on foot from the towns. When Jesus landed and saw a large crowd, he had compassion on them and healed their sick.
>
> As evening approached, the disciples came to him and said, "This is a remote place, and it's already getting late. Send the crowds away so they can go to the villages and buy themselves some food."
>
> Jesus replied, "They do not need to go away. You give them something to eat."
>
> "We have here only five loaves of bread and two fish," they answered.
>
> "Bring them here to me," he said. And he directed the people to sit down on the grass. (Matthew 14:13-19)
>
> Then after praying and giving thanks to His Father, Jesus broke the bread into pieces and gave them to the disciples to pass around to the people. Everyone had more than enough. In fact, they had leftovers—twelve baskets full (Matthew 14:19-20).

And from there, if that wasn't enough for one day, Jesus dismissed the crowd, sent His disciples ahead by boat, and hiked up a mountain alone to pray. Sometime during the night, He looked out on the lake and saw the boat bouncing along in the wind. He went out to it, walking on the water to His men. They were terrified. They thought, like we would, it must be a ghost, and they cried out in fear.

Immediately Jesus said, "Take courage! It is I. Don't be afraid."

Peter was quick to trust and said, "Lord, if it's you, tell me to come to you on the water."

Jesus said, "Come."

Peter got out of the boat and started walking toward Jesus on the water full of confidence, full of faith, then full of himself. When he saw the wind, he was afraid. He started sinking. He cried out, "Lord, save me!"

Jesus reached out His hand and caught him. "You of little faith," He said, "why did you doubt?" (Matthew 14:27-31)

In other words, why did you take your eyes off me? You were doing so well. Why did you look down, Peter? And to us He says the same: Why are you looking at your circumstances when I am sovereign over your circumstances? Why are you afraid when my hand is reaching out for yours?

This was a turning point in the lives of the disciples. As soon as Jesus and Peter climbed back into the boat, the wind died down.

Night On The Sea Of Galilee

The disciples were awestruck. They worshiped Him and said, "Truly you are the Son of God" (Matthew 14:33).

Were they really beginning to comprehend this humanly inconceivable truth? It was time to test them. Jesus took them to Caesarea Philippi in northern Galilee. With the shrine to the pagan god Pan—where human sacrifices were offered—in the background, He asked them point-blank who they thought He was.

THE SCENE TODAY

The Bible records **the conversation:**

Jesus asked his disciples, "Who do people say the Son of Man is?"
They replied, "Some say John the Baptist; others say
Elijah; and still others, Jeremiah or one of the prophets."

"But what about you?" he asked. "Who do you
say I am?"

Simon Peter answered, "You are the Christ, the Son
of the living God." (Matthew 16:13-16 [Mark 8:27-29])

Many people had started out with Jesus, anxious to see what He
would do next. But the harder His teaching became, the more they
fell away (John 6:66). To hear Peter say, "You are the Christ, the Son
of the living God," on the very spot where pagan gods were worshiped for centuries—dead gods that could neither think, hear, speak,
nor save—must have been very encouraging to Jesus. His Person
and His message had broken through to at least these few disciples.

The Bible says **Jesus told Peter:**

"Blessed are you, Simon son of Jonah, for this was not
revealed to you by man, but by my Father in heaven. And
I tell you that you are Peter, and upon this rock I will

91

build my church, and the gates of Hades will not overcome it." (Matthew 16:17-18)

God initiates our faith and expands our mind, stirs our heart, and
awakens our soul to understand and respond. Peter's response here
is a perfect example.

The Future

From that day forth, everyone who believed Jesus and chose to
follow Him would belong to His church. It would be formally insti-
tuted at Pentecost, after His death and resurrection, when the Holy
Spirit would come to live in believers (Acts 2). But for now, the foundation had to be laid. It was laid on Peter's statement of faith, "You
are the Christ, the Son of the living God."

Because Jesus brought heaven down here when He lived among
us and changed the world and all of history with His teaching, we
have this truth to look forward to: **Jesus is returning to establish
His kingdom on earth.**

What a glorious day that will be when peace will reign on planet
Earth! Think of it—no terrorist threats and no more scary epidemics
like Ebola. Those are our greatest fears today. Who knows what they
will be tomorrow. But when Jesus comes back to reign, there will
finally be peace.

Jesus draws us into His kingdom now, so we can catch the vision
of what that future looks like.

In the Meantime

We live in a world that eliminates moral absolutes, edits Scripture
to our liking, dethrones God, and creates its own personal religions.
But Jesus stands strong in the midst of it all and says the same to us
as He did those first disciples, "Come follow me!"

Maybe it's not in the middle of a storm. Maybe it's not in a hospital room or in the midst of another crisis. Maybe it's just in the
ordinary, routine, mundane that we sense our emptiness, our unhap-
piness, our deepest fear, our desperate need for so much more than
we've settled for.

That's exactly why Jesus makes it so clear who He is:

- "I am the bread of life."
- "I am the light of the world."
- "I am the gate."
- "I am the Good Shepherd."
- "I am the resurrection and the life."
- "I am the way and the truth and the life."
- "I am the vine."
- "And before Abraham was born, I am."
  Scripture references: John 6:48; John 9:5; John 10:9; John 10:14; John 11:25; John 14:6; John 15:5; John 8:58.

Everything we need and aspire to is found in Jesus Christ. He makes His identity perfectly clear. He is the eternal God of the universe. He had no beginning and He will have no ending. And His greatest desire is to lead us into a relationship with Him, because only in that relationship will we find the resources we need to live with joy and purpose in our constantly changing world.

Jesus' words brought strength and comfort to His first disciples, and they bring strength and comfort to us today.

The Bible says **Jesus** said:

"Come to me, all you who are weary and burdened, and I will give you rest. Take my yoke upon you and learn from me, for I am gentle and humble in heart, and you will find rest for your souls. For my yoke is easy and my burden is light." (Matthew 11:28-30)

Life in the twenty-first century makes us weary. It is burdensome and stressful. We make it that way. Between our need to be constantly busy and our desire to be constantly connected, is there any downtime to just rest? But rest isn't found in taking a nap, a walk, or a vacation. The rest Jesus is talking about is rest for our souls. Our souls are the inner part of us, the true part of us, the spiritual part of us, the part that will live on forever, long after our bodies are buried or cremated. They need refreshment. And it can only come from one source, our Creator. Jesus knows that, so He says: Link up with Me. Attach yourself to Me like you attach a yoke to your ox. My yoke is easy. It doesn't chafe and it's not heavy. We'll make a good team.

I'll make your journey easier and your work meaningful. Life will be better, together!

In that relationship, Jesus trains us just like He did the disciples, layer upon layer, until we are prepared to take the same test and answer the same question, "Who do you say I am?" And answer as Peter did, "You are the Christ, the Son of the living God."

Then our focus shifts from serving ourselves to serving Him, just like it did with Peter and the others. Within a few short years, they went from being just ordinary guys to being extraordinary forces for God and His kingdom. Peter became the head of the early church and spoke boldly to thousands of people.

The Bible says **Peter said:**

"Repent and be baptized, every one of you, in the name of Jesus Christ for the forgiveness of your sins. And you will receive the gift of the Holy Spirit. The promise is for you and your children and for all who are far off—for all whom our Lord our God will call."(Acts 2:38-39)

The church exploded. The Jewish leaders couldn't stop it. Rome couldn't stop it. Satan himself couldn't stop it. It continues on today, two thousand years later and counting. And we can be part of that.

Personal Reflection

Jesus still calls people the same way He did then. But He is seeking followers not just believers. There is a difference. To follow means: to stick with, to trust, to imitate, to obey.

One of the greatest privileges I had while teaching the Bible was witnessing this in women's lives. I saw God's power change belief systems that had been established since birth. For many this meant drastic consequences—they were willing to be disowned by their parents and cut off from their inheritance because of their new faith in Jesus Christ. They weren't content to just be silent and secret believers but boldly stepped forward to follow Him and trust Him with the results. Having never been in that position myself, I can't imagine the grief of that loss, but it was evident by their demeanor that what they gained in their new relationship with Jesus was worth it. And over time, many of these women were able to share their new faith with their families, and more lives were changed and relationships were restored as a result.

While Waiting His Return

Believing is the first step. Following is moving forward, one step at a time, with the goal of becoming more like Jesus. We are His hands and feet and voice in a fallen and broken world before He returns to establish His kingdom on earth.

Have you made your move into God's kingdom?

Would He consider you a believer or a follower?

Are you willing to change your status?

Where is He calling you to serve Him?

How have you responded?

How has your life changed as a result?

This hymn describes our need and God's solution.

Just as I am, without one plea
But that Thy blood was shed for me,
And that Thou bidd'st me come to Thee,
O Lamb of God, I come! I come!

Just as I am and waiting not
To rid my soul of one dark blot,
To Thee whose blood can cleanse each spot,
O Lamb of God, I come! I come!

Just as I am, though tossed about
With many a conflict, many a doubt,
Fightings and fears within, without,
O Lamb of God, I come! I come!

Just as I am Thou wilt receive,
Wilt welcome, pardon, cleanse, relieve.
Because Thy promise I believe,
O Lamb of God, I come! I come!
("Just as I Am" by Charlotte Elliott)

Now let's follow Jesus to Jerusalem.

PART II

JESUS COMPLETES HIS WORK

Chapter 7

Condemned in Jerusalem
Returning as Judge

*G*oing to Israel with my twenty-four-year-old granddaughter was indeed the trip of a lifetime. The first question everyone asks after such an experience is, "What was the high point for you; what made the greatest impression?"

We both agreed, it was going "up" to Jerusalem.

Our tour bus made its way south through the lush hills of Galilee into the barren landscape of Judea. The road seemed to stretch on forever, slowly climbing, climbing, climbing until suddenly, there in the distance, we saw it. Jerusalem. The silhouette of Jerusalem is unmistakable. It stands out like no other city in the world.

The Promise

Jerusalem is also known as the City of David and Zion. But most importantly it is God's city, the city of the Great King, the place He chose as His dwelling place (Psalm 48:2, 76:2).

> **Here's the promise:** Jesus is returning to His city, Jerusalem, to bring justice to earth.

JERUSALEM TODAY

The Past

Jesus had made the trip to Jerusalem numerous times in His life, certainly once a year to celebrate Passover with other Jewish pilgrims not only from Israel but neighboring nations as well. It was required by Jewish Law. The journey was arduous to say the least. They certainly didn't have the luxury of an air-conditioned, state-of-the-art tour bus, with plush seats, tinted windows, and beautiful music from the latest worship CD to insure they arrived rested and ready for the festivities. Families would walk the distance no matter how long it took or what dangers they had to pass through to get there. To give us some perspective, from Nazareth to Jerusalem would probably take three days on foot.

Jesus was going there now. This would be His last week on earth.

Two powerful events had just taken place that would prepare His disciples for what was coming and strengthen them after He died.

The first event was a vision of Jesus' divine nature. The second event demonstrated His power over death. Both would be carefully recorded so we, too, can have the same assurance they had of Jesus' identity, power, and purpose. Therefore, it is crucial that we understand their significance.

The first event occurred six days after Peter's bold acknowledgement that Jesus is the Christ, the Son of the living God (Matthew

16:16). Jesus took Peter, along with James and John, to a high mountain where He was literally transfigured before them, showing them His divine glory in the presence of two Old Testament saints, Moses and Elijah, no less. And once again they heard God's voice of approval.

***The Bible says* they heard:**
> "This is my Son, whom I love; with him I am well pleased. Listen to him!" (Matthew 17:5)

The three disciples were thunderstruck. They fell face down, terrified. Who wouldn't be? Jesus immediately reassured them. But later He used the opportunity to tell the rest of the disciples about His forthcoming death and resurrection. They were filled with grief, even though they couldn't possibly comprehend the significance of what He was saying. Jesus would tell them in different ways at different times with the same result.

Meanwhile, the second event happened in Bethany, less than two miles from Jerusalem. Jesus' good friends, Mary and Martha, sent word that their brother, Lazarus, was sick, very sick. Jesus had spent much time with this dear family. Their home was a place of refuge and rest during His ministry. They were generous in their love and hospitality to Him. So it was only natural they would send for Him now in this hour of distress. He sent word back to them assuring them Lazarus would not die.

The Bible says:
> "This sickness will not end in death. No, it is for God's glory so that God's Son might be glorified through it." (John 11:4)

But Lazarus did die.

And to make matters worse, Jesus procrastinated in going to be with the sisters. Four days went by. Finally He arrived and rather nonchalantly at that. Both women met Him with the same admonishment, "If you had been here, my brother would not have died" (John 11:21, 11:32).

Jesus responds with the greatest words any of us will ever hear.

The Bible says Jesus said:

"I am the resurrection and the life. He who believes in me will live, even though he dies; and whoever lives and believes in me will never die. Do you believe this?" (John 11:25-26)

Martha said YES! She believed He was the Christ, but could He really raise her brother from the dead?

The family, with many friends, went to the tomb where Lazarus was buried. Jesus stood there and wept. Death is so beyond our ability to understand and accept—and so final! Jesus wept, because we weren't supposed to die.

So He went over to the tomb, with its massive stone covering the entrance, and said, "Take away the stone!" Martha, the practical one, hesitated and said something about the odor. Jesus persisted.

The Bible says He said:

"Did I not tell you that if you believed, you would see the glory of God?" (John 11:40)

The stone was removed. Jesus prayed, thanking God for everyone to hear, then He called out in a loud voice, "Lazarus, come out!"

Lazarus came out, all wrapped up and bound in his grave clothes. What a picture it must have been. We can feel the suspense and hear the gasps as Jesus tells them to unwrap him and let him go. They did! Lazarus was alive (John 11:43-44).

Lazarus' resurrection prepared the world for what was to come for Jesus and for us!

Following these two demonstrations of His divine power, Jesus would enter His city, Jerusalem, on a lowly donkey and subject Himself in humility and obedience to God's plan on our behalf. What a contrast this gives us, as we see the two extremes of His nature. One reveals His divine nature as God; the other reveals His human nature as God in the flesh, willing to go forward to make eternal salvation possible for all mankind.

THOUGHT TO BE LAZARUS' TOMB

Now Jesus was ready for this most important week in all of history.
He sent two disciples on ahead to secure a donkey to ride into the city. The news was out. The crowds were ready. They took palm branches and went out to meet Him. They greeted Him with these words prophesied hundreds of years before.

The Bible says they shouted:
> "Hosanna! Blessed is he who comes in the name of the Lord! Blessed is the King of Israel!" (John 12:13)

The word "hosanna" means save. Jesus was fulfilling Psalm 118:25-26. He also fulfilled what the Old Testament prophet Zechariah said.

The Bible says:
> Rejoice greatly, O Daughter of Zion! Shout, Daughter of Jerusalem! See, your king comes to you, gentle and riding on a donkey, on a colt, the foal of a donkey. (Zechariah 9:9)

Everyone was asking the obvious. Who is this? Jerusalem was about to be shaken to its very foundation. Jesus went straight to the temple, not to worship, but to avenge, because pilgrims were exploited when they came in droves to buy their animals to sacrifice. The money changers charged exorbitant rates to convert their coins to Jewish shekels. Jesus was furious! He took a whip in His hands, went through, and literally chased them all out, scattering mountains of coins and knocking over tables in the process. No one had ever seen this side of Him.

What happened to that totally calm and in control man they had gravitated to and followed? Jesus didn't waste the opportunity to tell them.

The Bible says Jesus said:

"Is it not written: 'My house will be called a house of prayer for all nations'? But you have made it 'a den of robbers.'" (Mark 11:17)

From there, Jesus went about the city teaching.

After four hundred years of silence, God broke the silence and entered our world in human form. The writers of the four gospel accounts add different details and different timing, proving the authenticity of their records. Their accounts confirm each other while reflecting the different styles and personalities of the authors.

It is worth our noting the differences.

Matthew

Matthew, the tax collector, became Matthew the Apostle who wrote the Gospel of Matthew, the first book of the New Testament.

Matthew's purpose is to prove that Jesus is God, the promised Messiah. He does so in a very orderly fashion, much like our tax accountant lays out the facts for us at tax time. Matthew provides necessary information about the bloodline to prove Jesus' credentials and then carefully organizes His life and teachings by topics rather than in chronological order.

All these genealogical records were destroyed seventy years later when the Romans took over Jerusalem and burned the temple to the ground. This made it impossible for anyone else to claim they were the promised Messiah.

Mark

Mark's approach is different.

It's like he was writing with the twenty-first-century reader in mind. He gets right to the point and gives us the facts. He covers the events of Jesus' life with fewer words and less commentary than any of the other writers. He captures our attention with his fast-paced style and makes it very clear that the most dramatic event imaginable has occurred on planet Earth.

Luke

Luke was a physician by profession so his style is different yet.

He begins his account of Jesus' life with the Christmas story, Jesus' birth in Bethlehem. Joy erupted as heaven exploded with angels singing to welcome the newborn King. His royal birth literally split history in two. We confirm it every time we write the date. BC was before Christ. AD or *anno Domini* in Latin, separates now from then. The "year of our Lord" moved history in a new direction. Luke wants us to celebrate that every day! His writing reflects it.

John

John was one of the first disciples to be called. He later became known as the Apostle John who not only wrote the fourth Gospel account of Jesus' life but also three epistles or letters to the early church, as well as the last book of the Bible, Revelation.

John presumes we already know the facts and events surrounding Jesus' life. So he chooses instead to focus on the meaning of His life. He presents Jesus as the Word, or God's total expression of Himself, so there can be no mistake that He is indeed God in the flesh. Therefore, there can also be no mistake about why we should believe and follow this One who came to live among us and die for us.

Each of these writers add to our understanding of Jesus' final week on earth. The clock was ticking. Time was running out. Opposition was mounting and Jesus' followers still had so much to learn.

There was hardly a subject Jesus didn't address in those final few days as He traveled freely through the streets of His city teaching.

He thought nothing of offending His audience. He knew the religious leaders were out to trip Him up, so they'd have reason to get rid of Him. If they could bait Him to say forthrightly that He was God, that would be blasphemy, punishable by death.

But Jesus is in control of the events and the time, not them. So try as they will, He prevails.

His voice continues to speak out as He tells His audience the greatest commandment.

The Bible says **Jesus said:**

"'Love the Lord your God with all your heart and with all your soul and with all your mind.' This is the first and greatest commandment. And the second is like it: 'Love your neighbor as yourself.' All the Law and the prophets hang on these two commandments." (Matthew 22:37-40)

This alone infuriated the religious leaders. They thought they were above the Law that God had established, and they proved it by adding hundreds of their own to burden the people instead of helping them live the way God wanted them to for their own safety and well-being.

God hates spiritual hypocrisy and spiritual pride. Therefore, Jesus boldly and publically rebuked these leaders. They had disregarded the prophets that came before them, they had misled the people, and they had refused to recognize Jesus as the long promised Messiah and accept His teachings (Matthew 23:13-33). In fact, they were set on their course to destroy Him. They were just waiting for the first opportunity. They had to be careful, however, because the people loved Jesus. They hung on every word He said and continued to bring their sick to be healed.

Everything Jesus did was good.

But He was a marked man, and His time was running out. Within a matter of hours, He would be condemned to death. Even the crowd that welcomed Him with their "hosannas" on Sunday would be yelling, "Crucify Him!" on Friday.

The Future

In the midst of this mounting opposition, Jesus looks out at the city He loves so much and speaks to the future.

ANOTHER VIEW OF JERUSALEM TODAY

The Bible says:

"O Jerusalem, Jerusalem, you who kill the prophets and
stone those sent to you, how often I have longed to gather
your children together, as a hen gathers her chicks under
her wings, but you were not willing. Look, your house
is left to you desolate. For I tell you, you will not see
me again until you say: 'Blessed is he who comes in the
name of the Lord.'" (Matthew 23:37-39)

As Jesus walked past the temple, He used it as an illustration that
nothing we build with our own hands or value over Him will last.

The Bible says **He said:**

"Do you see all these things?" he asked. "I tell you the
truth, not one stone here will be left on another, every
one will be thrown down." (Matthew 24:2)

The disciples must have been thinking, how can that be? The
temple was built to last forever. But they knew better at this point
than to question Him so they simply asked the obvious, when will
this happen? (Matthew 24:3)

And Jesus seemed to look down through the ages to that time when sin will be so rampant on planet Earth that God will say, enough is enough! And He will bring history as we know it to an end. It's known as the End Times or the Day of the Lord. Many Bible scholars and believers in general who study the Bible believe we are there.

Jesus describes it as a time of
- spiritual confusion, complacency and apathy; people will be deceived by false teachers because they don't know Scripture;
- unprecedented violence and terror around the world;
- increasingly frequent natural disasters;
- brutal breakdown within families;
- unleashed hatred for anything representing God;
- unequaled anxiety and distress;
- unparalleled deception within the church;
- mounting persecution of believers;
- testing for even the most ardent followers of Jesus Christ;
- unmasked rebellion, self-centeredness, arrogance, greed, and pride.
  (from Matthew 24 and Mark 13)

But Jesus is jolted back to the present when the disciples ask how they will know when this will happen (Matthew 24:3). It is a question we're still asking today. We'll see His answer in the last chapter, but suffice it to say here that the second coming of Jesus Christ will be a stark contrast to His first coming.

He came the first time to save. He'll come the second time to judge.

Why wouldn't He? We've certainly had plenty of time and more than enough proof that He is God in the flesh, who laid His glory aside to come down here and rescue us from ourselves.

So what does judgment look like?

The Bible describes it as a time of reckoning, a time of accountability, a time when justice will be served. The whole world will be held accountable to having the presence of God in our midst.

Jesus has been given the authority to judge. Therefore, He will judge every nation and every individual on earth (John 5:22).

The Bible says:

"When the Son of Man comes in his glory, and all the angels with him, he will sit on his throne in heavenly glory. All the nations will be gathered before him, and he will separate the people one from another as a shepherd separates the sheep from the goats. He will put the sheep on his right and the goats on his left.

Then the King will say to those on his right, 'Come, you who are blessed by my Father; take your inheritance, the kingdom prepared for you since the creation of the world...

Then he will say to those on his left, 'Depart from me, you who are cursed, into the eternal fire prepared for the devil and his angels. ...'" (Matthew 25:31-34, 25:41)

The line of separation will be drawn. There will be no turning back.

We were created to have fellowship with God but sin denies us that privilege. God has provided salvation from sin and, therefore, reconciliation with Himself through Jesus Christ. He has given us every opportunity to know Him and come to Him. If we refuse this offer, we deserve eternal judgment because remember...

The Bible says:

"For God so loved the world that he gave his one and only Son, that whoever believes in him shall not perish but have eternal life." (John 3:16)

So we need Jesus, because even though He would soon be condemned to die a despicable death, the truth is: **Jesus is returning as Judge.**

Jesus will bring justice to planet Earth and even nature will rejoice.

The Bible says:

Then the trees of the forest will sing, they will sing for joy before the Lord, for he comes to judge the earth. (1 Chronicles 16:33)

In the Meantime

This chapter gives us the information we need to understand that someday we will all stand before God and be held accountable for our lives. When we do, we will either be declared guilty or not guilty. In God's court of Law, justified means to be declared not guilty because the blood of Jesus covers us. So instead of seeing our sin, God sees the blood of His Son. Therefore, His wrath and judgment pass over us just like the angel of death passed over the Israelites in Egypt when they had put the blood of the lamb on their doorpost (Exodus 12:1-13).

Without the blood of Jesus, there is no escaping His wrath and subsequent judgment on sin. He hates sin but loves the sinner. Every day our time on this earth is getting shorter.

We live in the most amazing, exciting, and challenging time in history. But it's also the most dangerous, seductive, and desperate time in history. We have amassed so much information it's impossible to stay abreast of it all. But the Word of God stands firm forever. So we can trust Jesus is coming and coming soon.

Personal Reflection

My father had what you could call a "last minute" conversion. He had lived his life about as far from God as anyone possibly could. He had exhausted his time, energy, and resources on empty pursuits. But when diagnosed with terminal cancer in his early seventies, he finally realized he had nothing to show for it. All he had in their place was a pile of debt and broken relationships.

That's when I got the call to come see him. He was the consummate businessman. He wanted the facts, the bottom line. What were his options? How could he ever approach God? I told him Jesus made it possible, and He was waiting for him to repent of his sins and come to Him.

Then I had the great privilege of watching this tall, dignified, prideful man fold his hands like a little child and with tears in his eyes say, "Dear Jesus, my name is Jennings Brown"—and then proceed to go through his life and take responsibility for his sin before our holy God. The best transaction he ever made. Three months later he was dead in this world but alive in the next.

It is a powerful experience to witness a flailing and desperate human being rescued and saved for all eternity by the Lord Jesus Christ.

While Waiting His Return

How will it be for you when Jesus comes either at your death or at the Rapture?

When you stand before Him, will He be your Justifier or your Judge?

You can make today the day of your salvation. Then you can look forward to His return with great joy and gratitude, instead of dread it with great fear and regret. Make every day count like Jesus did. Stop looking in the rearview mirror at your past failures, and live from here on out so you die with no regrets, because you are safe in the arms of Jesus.

This hymn is a beautiful prayer.

> Rock of Ages, cleft for me, let me hide myself in Thee;
> Let the water and the blood, from Thy wounded side which flowed,
> Be of sin the double cure, save from wrath and make me pure.
>
> Could my tears forever flow, could my zeal no languor know,
> These for sin could not atone; Thou must save and Thou alone.
> In my hand no price I bring; simply to Thy cross I cling.
>
> While I draw this fleeting breath, when my eyes shall close in death,
> When I rise to worlds unknown and behold Thee on Thy throne,
> Rock of Ages, cleft for me, let me hide myself in Thee.
> ("Rock of Ages" by Augustus M. Toplady)

Now let's move on to Thursday of Jesus' last week and go with Him to the Upper Room and His famous Last Supper on this earth.

Chapter 8

Last Supper in the Upper Room
Returning to Fulfill Prophecy

*I*f Jesus sent you an email saying He wanted to come to your house for dinner tonight, how would you respond to His request? Very few people had that unique opportunity during His ministry. Now He was looking for a place where He and His disciples could celebrate Passover. It had to be just the right place. This would be their last meal together. An unnamed "friend" got the privilege.

THOUGHT TO BE THE UPPER ROOM

The Promise

We don't know anything about this "friend" except that he was ready and willing to accommodate Jesus. And Jesus knew it.

The Bible says **Jesus told His disciples:**

"Go into the city to a certain man and tell him, 'The Teacher says: My appointed time is near. I am going to celebrate the Passover with my disciples at your house.'" (Matthew 26:18)

Here's the promise: Jesus controls all things — even time.

This was true in the past, and it will be true in the future. All prophecy recorded in the Bible will be fulfilled when Jesus returns.

It is crucial we believe this great truth before moving forward to the cross. Otherwise Jesus becomes just a "victim" of our brutality. On the contrary, He controlled His destiny here for our benefit. He placed Himself in just the right place at just the right time, the Jewish Passover, because He is our Passover lamb. Therefore, the meal itself has special significance.

The Past

Preparing the Passover meal was no easy feat. It required thought and preparation. The menu was always the same, commemorating the Israelites escape from Egypt. It included the Passover lamb, which had to be purchased and then kept for several days before being slaughtered and prepared for roasting. It also included bread made without yeast to remember the haste with which they had to leave.

So this most special feast day in the Jewish year was also called the Feast of Unleavened Bread. Thousands of pilgrims had converged upon the city, many camping out and cooking their meal over an open fire. But Jesus needed privacy. He had precious little time with His disciples, and He had quite an agenda.

To His disciples' surprise, Jesus began the evening by putting a towel around His waist and telling them that instead of a slave or a hired servant washing their feet, as was the custom, He would. They were confused. Peter objected, but Jesus insisted. Once again He was turning the world right side up by realigning their thinking with His. Instead of being served, He told them, it is you who are to serve. They submitted, not really understanding what they were submitting to, except for one.

Judas Iscariot hadn't signed up for this! He was looking for a totally different outcome to what he had given up to follow Jesus. He thought he would be part of Jesus' special cabinet to liberate Israel from Roman tyranny. Judas thought they'd all be heroes, not servants. At this point in time, he wanted action. So for whatever reason, he went to the authorities and made arrangements to betray Jesus. He made sure the religious leaders knew exactly where He was in the midst of the huge crowds. Judas would just wait patiently for the right time (Luke 22:1-6).

Is there anything worse than being betrayed by a friend, a spouse, a family member, a business partner? Once trust is broken, it's hard to reclaim. Only time and changed behavior restores it. Even though Jesus knew one of His men would betray Him, it did not have to be Judas. Judas had to succumb to the temptation Satan was proposing to him. This was the beginning of the "opportune time" Satan had been waiting for. He just needed a willing instrument to help him get it started.

Jesus didn't buckle under the disappointment or back away from His commitment.

The Bible says:
> Having loved his own who were in the world, he now showed them the full extent of his love. (John 13:1)

Jesus proceeded to go around the room and wash each man's feet, including Judas'. What kind of love is this, that even reaches out to someone He knows is against Him? It's hard enough to lead a group that you know is one hundred percent behind you, but dissension always undermines and threatens the success of any operation. Jesus was giving Judas a choice here: to accept Jesus' love and move forward together on His agenda or believe Satan's lie and follow his. Judas chose the latter.

Even so, Jesus continued with the Passover meal. It was His desire to give His followers from every nation, race, culture, language, and generation going forward, a universal sign of their oneness in Him.

In the midst of the meal, *the Bible says:*

> While they were eating, Jesus took bread, gave thanks and broke it, and gave it to his disciples, saying, "Take and eat; this is my body." Then he took the cup, gave thanks and offered it to them, saying, "Drink from it, all of you. This is my blood of the covenant, which is poured out for many for the forgiveness of sins. I tell you, I will not drink of this fruit of the vine from now on until that day when I drink it anew with you in my Father's kingdom." (Matthew 26:26-29 [Mark 14:22-25; Luke 22:18])

This meal would later be called Holy Communion, The Eucharist, or The Lord's Supper. But the purpose was the same — to remember Jesus and the sacrifice He was about to make on our behalf. What did the disciples think? What could they think? Even though Jesus had told them on numerous occasions that He was going to die, they had no idea when, how, or even why it would happen. And they certainly had no idea of what it would mean for their own future, both on earth and for all eternity.

The church, since its inception, has celebrated this meal as a remembrance of what Jesus did on the cross. So this night in the Upper Room with these twelve men was a foretaste of His imminent death for the sins of the human race and the forgiveness He came to offer.

After His death, it would serve as a constant reminder and attitude adjuster to help believers focus on Him. From our perspective two thousand years later, we can see how this simple act has served to keep the Body of Christ alive and healthy.

This meal represented the New Covenant that replaced the Old Covenant.

So what did this covenant mean? What was it all about?

In the Bible, a covenant is a promise God made either to one person or to a group of people and always represented His relationship with us. It was, therefore, a binding oath that was either conditional or unconditional.

The first covenant God made was with Adam in the Garden of Eden. It was conditional, and God made the conditions very clear.

The Bible says God said:

"You are free to eat from any tree in the garden; but you must not eat from the tree of the knowledge of good and evil. ..." (Genesis 2:16-17)

God is the perfect parent. He didn't want man exposed to all the evil Satan was responsible for. So He laid down the law. But Adam and Eve broke the law, and therefore the covenant, by eating the forbidden fruit and as a result, they fell under its curse because God also said, "For when you eat of it you will surely die" (Genesis 2:17).

Now there was no going back. The damage was done. The covenant was broken. There was no restoration at this point. But God was about to act on our behalf. He introduced another covenant, the covenant of grace, or His undeserved favor toward us. And He promised to ultimately destroy Satan through the seed of the woman (Genesis 3:15), pointing directly to Jesus Christ as the only One who could rescue us from our self-determined fate.

God made an unconditional covenant with Abraham when He promised to make him into the nation through which this Savior, the Messiah, would come, and He did. Thankfully, Jesus' coming was not dependent on Abraham or any of his descendants—only God's commitment to His promise.

This is great news, because if there were conditions attached to this covenant, someone in the lineage would surely have messed it up, and Jesus would not have been born. And we would be without a Savior and without hope.

Later on, God promised to bless His chosen people, the Israelites, IF they would obey His commandments. Their history proves that to be true. All their ups and downs were directly related to either their obedience or their disobedience to God.

The same holds true for us, even though we live in the time of the New Covenant not the Old Covenant.

When we choose to obey God and follow His "manual," the Bible, our lives are blessed just knowing we are aligned with Him regardless of our circumstances.

This New Covenant Jesus was giving the human race on this particular night in the Upper Room was the fulfillment of all the covenant promises God made in the Old Testament. Jesus offers us a new approach to God. The bread He broke and gave to His disciples represented His body that would soon be broken for them and for us. The wine He shared with them represented His blood that would soon be shed for them and for us. This replaces the covenant of the law that demands perfection and therefore, could never be kept and condemns us in the process. The New Covenant is the complete embodiment of God's grace to fallen humanity.

So this event in the Upper Room proves God's immense love and commitment to those He created and demonstrates Jesus' willingness to go through with the sacrifice required to restore our relationship with Him.

But the sacredness of this moment and Jesus' example of service seemed to escape the disciples. They began to argue among themselves who would be the greatest in His kingdom (Luke 22:24). At the same time, they were aware that one of them would betray Him and were just hoping it wasn't them (Matthew 26:22).

Jesus gave Judas another chance to change his mind.

The Bible says **Jesus told the disciples:**
> "It is the one to whom I give this piece of bread when I
> have dipped it in the dish."... (John 13:26)

Judas chose to take the bread, so Jesus told him, "What you are about to do, do quickly" (John 13:27). Jesus dismissed him, and Judas went out into the darkness of the night with these words ringing in his ears: "Woe to that man who betrays the Son of Man! It would be better for him if he had not been born" (Mark 14:21).

What a contrast between the light Jesus gives and the darkness of Satan; between the love Jesus gives and the "love" the world offers.

Jesus tells us to follow Him into the light; Satan tells us to stay in the dark. Jesus tells us to love our enemies; the world tells us to get even.

Now there were only eleven men left. Were they ready to understand what Jesus wanted and needed them to remember? He made sure they would. He knew what was coming and where He was going, so He stuck to His agenda and launched into what could be called His Farewell Address.

John's account is like being there. He writes that Jesus told them:
- My purpose in coming will be accomplished in my death, and God will be glorified in the process.
- Love one another; this is how men will know you are my disciples.
- My departure is imminent; you can't follow now but you will later; don't let your hearts be troubled; my Father's house has many rooms; I'm going to prepare a place for you; if I go, I'll come back for you; I want you to be where I am.
- I am the way and the truth and the life; if you've seen me, you've seen the Father; I and the Father are one.
- The Holy Spirit is coming; He will comfort you, guide you, and teach you; He is the Spirit of truth; He will be my presence in you.
- You will do even greater things than you've seen me do; ask me for anything in my name, and I will do it.
- If you love me, keep my commandments; trust me, I am coming back; I'm telling you all this before I go so you will believe.
  (John 13-14)

And with that, Jesus told the eleven it was time to go. But it was way too much information for the men to process, so Peter protested and asked where He was going. Jesus made it clear that where He was going, Peter couldn't follow then, but he would later. Peter protested again and said, "But I'm ready to die for you." And Jesus said, "Really, Peter? The truth is before you hear a rooster crow in the morning, you will deny you ever even knew me, and not once, but three times" (John 13:37-38).

Before leaving the Upper Room, it is important to note that artists through the centuries have depicted this scene of the Last Supper—Jesus at the center of a long, low table, the disciples all reclining around Him, John on one side, Judas on the other. One chooses life, the other chooses death.

The same choice is available to us because of what Jesus Christ was about to do. The difference is we have two thousand years of additional proof that Jesus is who He claimed to be, and, therefore, we can believe that He controls all things, even time—past, present, and future. And we can rest in that assurance.

The Future

Someday, Jesus is coming back to make all things clear. The truth is: **Jesus is returning to fulfill prophecy.**

Everything He has promised will be completely revealed. Hundreds of Old Testament prophecies have already been fulfilled: at His birth as we saw in chapter 2; during His life and through His ministry as we saw in chapters 3-6; in His suffering and by His death and resurrection as we see in chapters 7-11. And all prophecy will find completion in His return as we will see at the end of our study in chapter 12. When Jesus returns, we will have no more doubt, no more questions, no more confusion, because we will experience the reality for ourselves.

In the Meantime

This scene in the Upper Room raises some interesting questions about our free will and God's sovereignty. If He is in control, do we really have a choice? How does our free will interact with God's will? Did Judas have a say in his actions or was he "appointed" by God to betray Jesus?

God provides the answer. He created us in His image (Genesis 1:27). Therefore, we are blessed with intellect, reason, conscience, will, and emotions. We are given the freedom and responsibility to make our own choices and decisions in life. He has given us everything we need to make the right choices: His Word, His promises, His Son, and His Spirit to show us the way. The rest is up to us. Otherwise, we would be mere puppets.

119

So don't feel sorry for Judas. Jesus knew one of the twelve would betray Him. It was prophesied centuries beforehand. But Judas is never named as the betrayer. He chose to betray Jesus. He chose to go down in history as the fulfillment of that prophecy. He left the Upper Room and went out into the darkness and later committed suicide. The eleven remaining disciples chose to stay with Jesus. They left the Upper Room singing hymns.

Personal Reflection

I grew up in Los Angeles and went to an all girls Catholic high school. It was the fifties—the days of saddle shoes and bobby sox; rock-and-roll music and milkshakes; Corvettes and Chevy Impalas. In a weak moment, my Dad bought me a red '55 T-bird to drive the thirty minutes back and forth to school. Life was good!

In the midst of this background, I had a significant spiritual experience. One of my classmates invited me to a party at her home in Beverly Hills. I was overjoyed; her father was a movie star. A few of us had spent our free time following the "Hollywood Guide to the Homes of Movie Stars" map, hoping to catch a glimpse or get an autograph. Now I was going to meet a real movie star, face-to-face. The house was unlike any I'd ever seen before or since: huge rooms; high ceilings; expansive gardens; incredible art work. The dining room was literally like walking into the "Upper Room." A life-size mural of the Last Supper adorned an entire wall. The father reverently described the scene to this suddenly subdued group of exuberant sixteen-year-olds: Jesus securing the room; Jesus washing the disciple's feet; Jesus preparing them for His death; Jesus instituting the Last Supper; Judas betraying Him. You could hear a pin drop. "How could Judas do that?" we all exclaimed in unison. Again the father used the opportunity as a teaching moment. "We all betray Jesus, he told us, when we refuse to follow Him and choose to go our own way instead."

All these years later that night stands out in my memory—not because of the beautiful home and the chance to meet a famous movie star, but because of his words that would help shape my thinking and, later, solidify my faith.

Thank God, Jesus left the Upper Room that night determined to carry out His mission on our behalf just as prophesied.

While Waiting His Return

Where do you stand in your own faith?

How determined are you to follow Jesus?

What is He asking you to do that He can count on you to do?

Where are you being tempted to do your own thing instead?

How do the events of the Upper Room help put things in perspective?

Are you willing to share your faith with someone else?

This hymn is a beautiful prayer of commitment.

Take my life and let it be consecrated, Lord to Thee;
Take my moments and my days; let them flow in ceaseless praise,
Let them flow in ceaseless praise.

Take my will and make it Thine; it shall be no longer mine;
Take my heart, it is Thine own; it shall be Thy royal throne,
It shall be Thy royal throne.
("Take My Life and Let It Be" by Frances R. Havergal)

Now let's follow Jesus to the Garden of Gethsemane.

Chapter 9

Agony in the Garden
Returning in Glory

*I*t's only natural to seek a place of comfort when we're hurting the most. For some, it's the ocean or the mountains or the woods. For others, it's a spa or favorite vacation spot or home. For Jesus, it was a garden just across the Kidron Valley from the Upper Room. He and His disciples had been there often. It was their quiet get-away, their retreat from the noisy streets of Jerusalem. Now, on the eve of Passover, it offered Him the seclusion He needed. It was actually an olive grove appropriately called Gethsemane, because Gethsemane means olive press. Jesus was about to be pressed to the limits of human capacity. He needed time and space to prepare. This was the perfect place.

THE GARDEN OF GETHSEMANE TODAY

The Promise

The Garden of Gethsemane was a defining time for Jesus, and indeed, for the whole human race. Jesus could have changed the course of history and left us without any hope of being reconciled to God. But because He made the decision to go forward on our behalf, in spite of the agony He knew He was facing, we can be sure that we will see Him return in glory.

We can't even find words to describe what His glory might look like, but we do know that it means seeing Jesus in the fullness of who He really is: we will see His radiant beauty, His majesty, His splendor, His holiness, His goodness, and His power. We will see Him just as He had been in heaven before coming to earth and just as He was when He returned to heaven after His resurrection. What a sight that will be!

> **Here's the promise:** We will see Jesus return in all His glory because He committed to the cross in Gethsemane.

The Past

Gethsemane was the "more opportune time" Satan referred to when he failed to tempt Jesus in the wilderness (see chapter 5). Gethsemane was Jesus' opportunity to turn from God's plan of redemption through His sacrifice and walk out of that garden free of the burden and free of the suffering. Every part of His humanity struggled with the decision. The ramifications were huge; heaven would be open to us if He went forward, closed if He did not. He chose to go forward.

Let's go with Him now in order to fully appreciate what He subjected Himself to for us.

After leaving the Upper Room, Jesus entered Gethsemane with the eleven remaining disciples. He told eight of them to stay behind and wait. Then He took Peter, James, and John with Him and told them to keep watch with Him. He knew at this very moment that Judas was leading the religious leaders to Him. Judas knew Gethsemane was Jesus' favorite place. Time was running out. Jesus went on ahead by Himself and fell with His face to the ground and prayed.

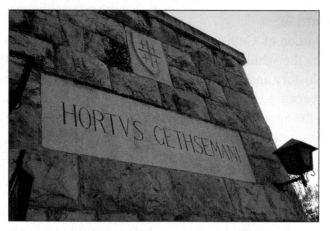

ENTRANCE TO GETHSEMANE TODAY

The Bible says Jesus said:

"My Father, if it is possible, may this cup be taken from me. Yet not as I will, but as you will." (Matthew 26:39)

What was Jesus asking and what is the cup?

In His humanity, Jesus knew the brutal and indescribable pain He was facing, but that was nothing compared to the incomparable pain of being separated from His Father. This would be the first time. Why? Because our sin, which separates us from God, would be placed on Him as our lamb, our sacrifice.

Just as the sins of the people were symbolically placed on the animal they brought to the temple to be slain on their behalf, so Jesus was going to be slain on our behalf. This would necessitate an unprecedented separation from His Father. Jesus literally became sin. Our iniquities were placed on Him (Isaiah 53:6). Therefore, God had to turn away from His own beloved Son until the sacrifice was complete. In the meantime, Jesus would experience God's wrath instead of His love. Our sin incurs His wrath, and rightfully so, because of what it has done to His creation.

This is the cup Jesus faced. His human side shuddered and begged for it to be removed. But His divine side knew that it was the only way that gap could be filled, that separation between God and man repaired. So He willingly accepted it.

But while He was praying and struggling with the full impact of this, even to the extent that His sweat actually became droplets of blood (Luke 22:44), Peter, James, and John were sleeping. We can't blame them. We could easily do the same. Jesus asked them twice to wake up and pray, but twice He returned and found them asleep. He reprimanded Peter.

The Bible says **Jesus said:**
"Watch and pray so that you will not fall into temptation. The spirit is willing, but the body is weak." (Matthew 26:41)

Within a matter of hours, Peter would find out just how true those words are, and every believer since has experienced the same.

Jesus left them sleeping and went off a third time to pray. Then He returned and roused them again.

The Bible says **Jesus said:**
"Are you still sleeping and resting? Look, the hour is near, and the Son of Man is betrayed into the hands of sinners." (Matthew 26:45)

The disciples' time with Jesus' physical presence was coming to an abrupt end. Judas was leading a large contingency of Roman soldiers into the garden. The designated signal to identify Jesus was a kiss, so Judas didn't hesitate to go right to Jesus and kiss Him. But this brutal act of betrayal wasn't even necessary, because Jesus was committed to His fate. He purposefully presented Himself to His captors with such dignity and majesty that they fell backward.

The Bible says:
So Judas came to the grove, guiding a detachment of soldiers and some officials from the chief priests and Pharisees. They were carrying torches, lanterns and weapons.

Jesus, knowing all that was going to happen to him, went out and asked them, "Who is it you want?"

"Jesus of Nazareth," they replied.

"I am he," Jesus said. (And Judas the traitor was standing there with them.) When Jesus said, "I am he," they drew back and fell to the ground. (John 18:3-6)

Was it Jesus referring to Himself as "I am" that made them fall to the ground? Over and over again in His teaching, He had made the connection between God calling Himself "I am" in the Old Testament (Exodus 3:14), and His own claims of identity in the New Testament (the "I am" statements talked about in chapter 6).

Or was it the glow of His majesty; the contrast between His humility and their arrogance; His love and their hate; the sense of His divine authority; or the gnawing conviction that He was indeed the Messiah that took them down?

But when they were able to get up and pull themselves together, Jesus was still standing there because He had accepted the cup of suffering to achieve our redemption. It was a defining moment in human history. Jesus was headed to the cross, and we would forever be the beneficiaries. We would have a way back to God.

OLDEST TREE IN GETHSEMANE TODAY

The Future

Until we understand what it cost Jesus to go to the cross, we will never understand the immense love God has for us. But we will also never understand the "end of the story," because Jesus may have left Gethsemane in disgrace as a human being, but the truth is someday: **He is returning in glory.**

It staggers our imagination and stretches our brain to even think about His glory, but now we know that it is seeing Jesus enveloped in all His splendor, majesty, holiness, and power that is rightfully His. But there is something more: Jesus will return not only with His original glory that He had in heaven as Son of God, but He will also have the additional glory as Son of Man because His mission on earth will have been accomplished. It is impossible to adequately describe or define this super amazing event, but everyone will experience it when He returns.

The Bible says:

...While we wait for the blessed hope—the appearing of our great God and Savior, Jesus Christ,..." (Titus 2:13)

"There will be signs in the sun, moon and stars. On the earth, nations will be in anguish and perplexity at the roaring and tossing of the sea. Men will faint from terror, apprehensive at what is coming on the world, for the heavenly bodies will be shaken. At that time they will see the Son of Man coming in a cloud with power and great glory." (Luke 21:25-27)

"When the Son of Man comes in his glory, and all the angels with him, he will sit on his throne in heavenly glory." (Matthew 25:31)

What an amazing future we have to look forward to! Realistically, we can't even imagine it. We just want to be absolutely sure we're on board—waiting and expecting Jesus' return in glory so we can rejoice in it and not be terrified by it.

In the Meantime

Jesus was prepared to face this adversity for our good. In our lives, too, adversity can lead to good when we turn to God and trust Him to navigate us through it and bring good from it. When we do, He proves His faithfulness, sovereignty, and unconditional love.

So will we accept what the Father has allowed in our lives? Or will we reject it because we think we deserve better; or we're entitled to more; or we lead good lives; or we didn't sign up for this? How we respond to this knowledge of what Jesus accomplished for us determines how we live in the present.

By our actions we are all related to someone in the Garden of Gethsemane when Jesus was betrayed:

- We stand with Judas, who has lived and worked with Jesus along with His other followers but in the end proves to be a fake; or
- We stand with the soldiers and the mixed crowd that had gathered, rejecting Him because of peer pressure, political correctness, religious self-righteousness, ignorance, or simply refusing to come out of the darkness into the light; or
- We stand with Jesus and believe the entirety of God's Word and His purpose in allowing His beloved Son to leave the glory of heaven and come down here to subject Himself to what He was facing now as He headed toward the cross.

Every day we choose our response to Jesus Christ; we either reject Him, neglect Him, ignore Him, or embrace Him. Which will it be? Every day is a new day and a new opportunity to see His power at work in us, fulfilling His purpose through us.

Personal Reflection

The Garden of Gethsemane represents the time we all need with God.

I have learned from experience how absolutely vital that time is. It resets my focus and recharges my batteries, so I have the strength and confidence to face life—and death, whenever and however that comes. The way Jesus prayed for Himself in Gethsemane and how

He acted afterwards has taught me the basic necessities for living my life with and for God.

I have found the first necessity is to pray. I figure if Jesus needed to pray, how much more do I. Prayer is our lifeline to God. I was so relieved when I learned that prayer does not have to be long, formal, complicated, or boring. Prayer is simply talking to God. Like any father, God loves it when we come to Him and just want to share our hearts with Him. So we can talk to God anytime, anywhere.

But I have also learned that it is extra beneficial to set aside a special time to pray each day. Structuring the time helps me stay focused. I begin with thinking about Him. God is holy, righteous, and trustworthy. He is sovereign, faithful, just, and merciful. He is also powerful, present, and unchangeable. He is the Alpha and the Omega, the beginning and the end, and He is coming again. Just repeating that much quiets my mind and reassures me that all will be well, because He is in control.

I know I need to take responsibility for my sins and confess them to God, because sin blocks my communication with Him. I make sure to ask Him to bring those things to mind that need to be confessed so He will forgive me and I can move forward. When I reminded our youngest daughter of our need to confess our sin and ask for God's forgiveness when she was little, she said, "Oh, I do that on my way home from school, because that's where I do all my bad things!" I need that same honesty when I pray. We all do "bad" things. We think bad thoughts, say bad things, and do bad things, and we need to confess them before a holy God. The Bible says when we do, God is faithful and just to forgive us (1 John 1:9). The slate is wiped clean, we're free to move on, and our guilt is replaced with joy.

Thanking God for all His blessings is also an important part of my prayers. It puts things in perspective. Everything I have comes from Him, and everything I have belongs to Him. When I recognize that truth, I become more aware of His goodness, and I find myself becoming even more grateful. Yet, sometimes it's easy to skip that part and bombard Him with my problems instead. With four married children and ten grandchildren, I can keep Him pretty busy with all of our needs. But then I remind myself that He knows my concerns and my circumstances, and as my Father, He loves me to bring them to Him so He can help me navigate through them. This increases my gratitude and gives me confidence as I watch Him work, and He gets the credit as He should.

Thinking about Jesus in Gethsemane, it's obvious that He did not stop with prayer. Prayer for Him led to obedience. This is a necessity that I keep learning with God's help. Life simply gets better when we align ourselves with Him. He designed it that way. That's why He gave us His Word, the Bible, to read and live by. We could call it our Owner's Manual. But like the stubborn Israelites in their long history of trying to do things their way, we often have to learn the hard way. We are all guilty of this, but my paternal grandfather provides a perfect example. Graduating from Yale while still a teenager, his life held great promise, yet it was wasted on alcohol, gambling, and women. Thank God he started reading the Bible in his eighties and died looking forward to eternity in heaven. In a few short years, he left his grandchildren a powerful legacy for which I have always been grateful.

Jesus' example in the Garden of Gethsemane also teaches me to trust God with my future. This too is a necessity. Knowing my future is secure with Him in heaven gives me confidence in the present. Some people insist that we cannot be sure we're going to heaven. My mother struggled with this most of her life, thinking it is presumptuous on our part. But accepting God's grace at His Son's expense is not presumptuous. It is letting go of our own insistence that we don't need to be saved or that we can somehow save ourselves. What a relief to know that Jesus went forward to the cross to pay the debt for our sin—in full. There is nothing we can add to that; it is a done deal. My mother is enjoying that reality now. And I look forward to enjoying it with her in the future.

While Waiting His Return

Now is the time to recognize our need, let go of our pride, and turn to Jesus like He turned to His Father in Gethsemane, so we too can experience His glory.

Where do you need to let Him have His way with you today?

What sin is keeping you from doing that?

How will knowing that Jesus prayed for you encourage you to pray?

Do you have a favorite time and place to pray?

This hymn makes a beautiful prayer.

Have Thine own way, Lord! Have Thine own way!
Thou art the Potter; I am the clay.
Mold me and make me after Thy will,
While I am waiting, yielded and still.
("Have Thine Own Way" by Adelaide A. Pollard)

Now we are ready to follow Jesus to the cross.

Chapter 10

Dying on the Cross
Returning as Proven Redeemer

The cross stands firmly established in the history of the human race as proof of what God has done on our behalf. Just as Jesus was forced to carry the heavy crossbeam to His place of execution, we carry the responsibility to respond.

The Promise

We all come to that crossroads in our lives. We all face the question, "what will I do with Jesus?" He went to the cross to save us the punishment and guilt that our sin deserves. His arrest, trials, and death are among the most studied, documented, illustrated, and proven events in history but also among the most unfair, illegal, and inhumane events in history. They represent our total depravity as human beings. And yet, the cross represents the immensity of God's love for us. The cross is where the two extremes meet. The cross is the intersection that offers us a new beginning, new opportunities, new hope, and a new future. This deserves a response.

As we revisit this powerful scene, may we catch a fresh vision of what it means that Jesus died in our place. And in the process, may we have the same passion for Him that He demonstrated for us on that cross. And may our lives continue to be changed as a result.

Here's the promise: Our lives are changed forever when we come to the cross.

The Past

Jesus' final twenty-four hours on this earth were brutal to say the least.

It is important we walk through them with Him, so we realize what our redemption cost Him and how it changes us.

It began in Gethsemane and ends in a grave, but the best news of all time is that is not the end of Jesus of Nazareth.

So let's look at the details of those hours with that in mind.

After Judas led the Roman soldiers and Jewish leaders to Jesus in the garden, soldiers arrested Him, bound Him, and led Him back through the now quiet streets of Jerusalem to the house of the high priest.

Only John records this first of six irregular "trials."

Before Annas

Annas was the first to interrogate Jesus. Even though he was retired and his son-in-law, Caiaphas, was now the official high priest, Annas hoped to be the one to implicate Jesus in anti-Roman activity that would merit His death. This would insure continued respect among his colleagues and favor from Rome.

So even though it was late and undoubtedly past his bedtime, Annas quickly made himself presentable and proceeded to question Jesus about His disciples and His teaching. Jesus questioned him in return.

The Bible says **Jesus replied:**

> "I have spoken openly to the world. I always taught in synagogues or at the temple, where all the Jews come together. I said nothing in secret. Why question me? Ask those who heard me. Surely they know what I said." (John 18:20-21)

This prompted one of the temple guards to step forward and hit Jesus in the face (John 18:22).

To which Jesus responded:

> "If I said something wrong, testify to it. But if I spoke the truth why did you strike me?" (John 18:23)

Apparently this was enough for Annas. He had made his appearance and had seen Jesus firsthand, so he sent Him on to Caiaphas.

Before Caiaphas

This second Jewish "trial" included some other members of the council called the Sanhedrin. By this time it was past midnight, so not everyone was there, but they were determined to make sure Jesus died. Threatening to destroy the temple and claiming to be God would do it. They called in false witnesses to testify, but none of their testimonies agreed, so finally Caiaphas questioned Jesus directly.

The Bible describes **their conversation:**

> The high priest said to him, "I charge you under oath by the living God: Tell us if you are the Christ, the Son of God."
>
> "Yes it is as you say," Jesus replied. "But I say to all of you: in the future you will see the Son of Man sitting at the right hand of the Mighty One and coming on the clouds of heaven." (Matthew 26:63-64)

That sealed Jesus' fate. The high priest tore his robe in disgust and the council condemned Him as worthy of death. They became a frenzied mob. After blindfolding Jesus, they hit Him, spit on Him, and taunted Him to prophesy who hit Him (Matthew 26:65-68). But it wasn't legal to try capital cases at night, so as soon as the first rays of daylight appeared and they could rouse the rest of the Sanhedrin, a third Jewish "trial" was held.

THE "PIT" WHERE IT IS THOUGHT JESUS WAS HELD

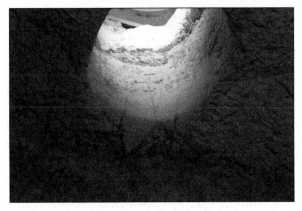

THE OPENING TO THE PIT

Before the Sanhedrin

The members of the Sanhedrin all agreed. The decision was unanimous; Jesus would die (Mark 14:64). There was only one problem. Only the Romans could put anyone to death (John 18:31). The Jews were under their authority.

So Jesus was taken to Pontius Pilate, the Roman governor of Judea at the time, for the first of three political "trials."

Before Pilate

Like the disciples from Galilee, Pilate had no idea when he woke up that morning that this day would change his life forever. Some days are like that. We have no idea what the next twenty-four hours hold or how the decisions we make then will affect us and everyone around us later.

Pilate had heard about Jesus and His claims to be a king. That didn't disturb him, however, because the Jews under his jurisdiction always seemed to have some sort of crisis. So at first he just tried to placate them and settle this matter as quickly and quietly as possible. But he soon realized that this was no ordinary case, and the prisoner standing before him was no ordinary man.

When Pilate asked Jesus if He was the King of the Jews, Jesus truthfully replied "yes!" But when the Jewish leaders accused Him of numerous false charges, Jesus was silent. Pilate was both perplexed and amazed. He sensed something different about Jesus. In fact, Pilate's wife even sent him a message telling him she had a dream about Jesus and to have nothing to do with Him. But Pilate was caught between a rock and a hard place.

It was the custom during the Passover to release one prisoner. So he thought surely the Jews would choose to release Jesus over the notorious murderer, Barabbas, being held in the Roman jail. But the crowd was egged on by the chief priests and insisted that Pilate release Barabbas instead (Matthew 27:11-21).

Pilate was running out of options. He knew Jesus was innocent, so he stated his verdict: "I find no basis for a charge against this man" (Luke 23:4).

The crowd wouldn't let up. They accused Jesus of stirring up trouble all over Judea, starting in Galilee. This gave Pilate another opportunity to spare Jesus. Being from Galilee meant He was under Herod's jurisdiction, and Herod just happened to be in Jerusalem. Pilate thought this would solve the Jesus problem as far as he was concerned. So he sent Him to Herod (Luke 23:5-7).

Before Herod

Herod was thrilled. He had heard about this "miracle worker" and hoped to see a few miracles himself, so he looked forward to seeing Jesus (Luke 23:8). But when Jesus stood before this great Roman ruler, all Herod saw was an exhausted, filthy, and pathetic-looking figure, who didn't look capable of defending Himself, much less threatening Rome. Herod still questioned Him, but not because he wanted to know the truth. Therefore, Jesus was silent before him (Luke 23:9). But Herod had to have his fun, so he and his soldiers ridiculed and mocked Jesus before dressing Him in an elegant robe befitting a king and sending Him back to Pilate (Luke 23:11).

Back to Pilate

Pilate thought he was done. But God was giving him yet another opportunity to do the right thing and release Jesus. Jesus was giving him every opportunity to see the light and respond. He knew Pilate was conflicted. So unlike with Herod, He gave Pilate more information.

The Bible records the dialogue:

> Jesus said, "My kingdom is not of this world. If it were, my servants would fight to prevent my arrest by the Jews. But now my kingdom is from another place."
>
> Pilate was curious and said, "You are a king then!"
>
> To which Jesus replied, "You are right in saying I am a king. In fact, for this reason I was born, and for this I came into the world, to testify to the truth. Everyone on the side of truth listens to me." (John 18:36-37)

Truth was standing right in front of Pontius Pilate that day, but he just shrugged his shoulders and asked what many people ask today, "What is truth *anyway*?" (John 18:38) We're only given so many opportunities to recognize the truth and align with it. Pilate made his choice that day. He went back out to the crowd and tried again to release Jesus instead of Barabbas. But the crowd drowned him out with their incessant cries, "Take Him away! Take Him away! Crucify Him!" Even though Pilate had insisted he could find no fault with Jesus, when the crowd accused him of not being a friend of Caesar, he finally gave in to their demands (John 19:15-16).

The Crucifixion

And so it was that Pilate released Jesus, first to be ridiculed by Roman soldiers and mockingly crowned as King of the Jews, and then flogged, hoping this might appease the Jews. But it didn't. So after the brutal scourging that often left the prisoner near death, Jesus was led out to be crucified. Pilate washed his hands, telling the people he was not responsible (Matthew 27:24). But from that day forward, his name would go down in history as the man who sentenced Jesus Christ to be crucified on a cross.

Standing just outside the walls of Jerusalem near the hill called Golgotha, or "place of the skull," takes us back to that day.

PICTURE OF GOLGOTHA TODAY

It's easy to imagine the throngs of people walking past this public place of execution. Since crucifixion was chosen by the Romans to deter any type of political insurrection, Jesus was nailed to a cross and hoisted into an upright position. A sign over Him identified Him as King of the Jews in three languages for everyone to see.

Untold numbers of books have been written, music composed, statues erected, symbols produced, paintings painted, and movies produced to depict the scene and permanently etch it into our memories.

But what was it like to be there?

We can know through the people involved. They offer us different perspectives.

The religious leaders were relieved! They had every reason and proof to receive Jesus as their Messiah because they had

- the Old Testament Scriptures;
- the prophecies concerning His arrival;
- the history of God's presence, beginning with Abraham;
- the Messiah's genealogy recorded through their people;
- all their traditions with the appointed laws, feast days and sacrifices that all pointed to Him; and
- hundreds of prophecies being fulfilled by Him.

Yet they rejected Jesus simply because He did not fulfill their expectations. They expected a royal king who would sweep them up in his kingdom and overthrow the Roman government, not a humble servant who would demand the same from them. And they were too set in their ways. They were too stubborn, too sophisticated, too well-educated (or so they thought), too elite, and too arrogant and prideful to change. But arrogance often comes from prideful ignorance. Meanwhile, after twenty centuries, their Messiah is still waiting for them—at the foot of the cross.

Two thieves were also crucified with Jesus that day.

Their perspective provides an interesting contrast. They had opposite backgrounds from the religious leaders. They were "down and outers," social outcasts, most likely uneducated and unrefined, with little or no knowledge of Jewish history, traditions, or prophecy. Yet they were given the special privilege of being crucified with the Savior. They reacted differently to the situation with very different results. One insulted Jesus and dared Him to get them all down if He really was the Messiah. The other took responsibility for his sins and defended Jesus (Luke 23:39-40).

The crowd offers us yet another perspective.

According to the tour guide on my trip, it's estimated that hundreds of people walked by Jesus that day during the six hours He hung there naked, bleeding, cramping, convulsing, and gasping for air.

What was their reaction?

It's the same as today; perhaps some were curious or even sympathetic. Undoubtedly others were indifferent, complacent, cynical, skeptical, passive, pre-occupied, self-absorbed, and just too busy to even stop and notice, let alone care. The rationale is the same as well: "What's that to me? I have a life to live, and I don't need God to help me!"

We can't help but wonder how many of those people that witnessed Jesus' death that day came back to the foot of the cross before they died.

Now let's look at Jesus' perspective. His seven statements reveal it for us to ponder. No sooner had the soldiers done their brutal duty and driven the iron stakes through His hands and feet, while others were mocking Him and gambling for His clothing, that Jesus uttered the following indelible words:

To the people
The Bible says **Jesus said:**
> "Father, forgive them, for they do not know what they are doing." (Luke 23:34)

This statement alone reveals Jesus' mission in going to the cross, for there would be no forgiveness without His sacrifice. But can you imagine being in such extreme pain and making everyone else your priority? We're included in the "everyone else," because our sins put Him there just as surely as those Roman soldiers. In fact, they had more of an excuse than anyone else at the time, or even now, not to understand what they were doing. They were just doing their job. They were paid executioners. To them, Jesus was just another enemy of the system that had to be put down. And crucifixion was guaranteed to scare the rebellious spirit out of anyone. But certainly they saw something very different in Jesus.

These words must have pricked their consciences. The question is, do they prick ours? Or has our indifference and our complacency and cynicism and skepticism and passivity and pre-occupation and self-absorption and just plain busyness hardened us to such an extent that we no longer feel and no longer care?

The Jews, on the other hand, had the greater responsibility because they did know what they were doing. Jesus had openly taught that He was the Messiah, and they had the Scriptures to prove it. But they ignored the light they had been given. Yet Jesus prayed these words for all people in every generation—those with no knowledge and those with much knowledge. His forgiveness is for everyone. But it's only available at the foot of the cross.

To the thief
Jesus' next statement was to one of the thieves who told the other thief to stop insulting Jesus.

The Bible says he wisely said:
> "Don't you fear God, since you are under the same sentence? We are punished justly, for we are getting what our deeds deserve. But this man has done nothing wrong." Then turning to Jesus, he said: "Remember me when you come into your kingdom." (Luke 23:40-42)

The Bible says Jesus replied:
> "I tell you the truth, today you will be with me in paradise." (Luke 23:43)

This man knew his need, recognized the Savior, confessed his sin, and received salvation—"today"! Think of it—no delay, no holding pattern, no time wasted, no test to pass, and nothing to prove. That very day, this thief would no longer be called an outsider or a down and outer, but a saint, redeemed by the blood of his Savior, because he bowed his heart to Him at the foot of the cross. The Apostle Paul describes it well: "Away from the body and at home with the Lord" (2 Corinthians 5:8).

The other thief refused to repent and died in his sins.

To His mother

Jesus' mother was standing nearby. Her heartbreak must have been unbearable. Jesus knew it. So did the disciple, John, who had overcome his fear enough to come and stand by her. Jesus looked at Mary with all the love of a son for his mother, who had given him birth and raised him to manhood.

The Bible says Jesus said:

"Dear woman, here is your son." (John 19:26)

And He looked at John with all the love of a shepherd for one of his frightened sheep and said:

"Here is your mother." (John 19:27)

To His Father

Then about noon, a great darkness came over the land. This was not a storm moving in or a heavy fog or blowing sand. It was a supernatural phenomenon that remains supernatural today. It was a foreboding darkness—a darkness that penetrated the whole land. The sun had stopped shining. It seemed like the light Jesus had brought into the world had been put out. This was the darkness of hell. Jesus had become sin for us. In the process, His Father had forsaken Him. He had to. He could not look on our sin. God represents all that is holy and pure. Sin represents everything that is unholy and impure. Jesus took all the sins of the human race—past, present, and future—and "descended into hell," as the early creed of Christian beliefs, the Apostle's Creed, affirms. Jesus felt this isolation and condemnation as He cried out in a loud voice.

The Bible says Jesus said:

"Eloi, Eloi, lama sabachthani?"—which means, "My God, my God, why have you forsaken me?" (Matthew 27:46)

We will never be able to fully comprehend His experience until we get to heaven, but Jesus made three more statements that help us know with certainty that He completed what He came to do. And God was satisfied.

Final words

We can't imagine the terrible thirst that Jesus experienced as His body was being drained of all its fluids. But in order to complete this work and make sure we knew that it was—

The Bible says Jesus said:

"I am thirsty." (John 19:28)

He was offered a sponge dipped in wine vinegar. This enabled Him to cry out in a loud voice, "It is finished" (John 19:30). And then say, "Father, into your hands I commit my spirit" (Luke 23:46).

Jesus' execution was not murder in the true sense of the word. This was Jesus, the Messiah, who had come into the world to save the world, *voluntarily* giving up His life so that we may have eternal life. He had controlled the events, the timing, and His death. Now it was finished! It was not a cry of surrender to His circumstances. It was a shout of victory on our behalf. Now it was possible for every human being, when facing death, to hear along with that thief: "Today you will be with me in paradise" (Luke 23:43).

Dozens of prophecies were fulfilled that day. Isaiah 53 and Psalm 22 describe these events in detail hundreds of years beforehand. But at the time, the earth itself reacted with a powerful earthquake. Rocks were split and graves were opened. Dead people were suddenly alive and later seen walking around. The heavy curtain inside the temple that, according to Jewish historians, was as thick as the palm of a man's hand and required three hundred priests to put in place, tore open from top to bottom (Matthew 27:51-53). The barrier between God and man had been removed.

The terrified Roman centurion in charge of Jesus' execution could only say, "Surely this man was the Son of God" (Matthew 27:54).

Jesus died that day for you and for me.

The Future

Jesus' life and death has had a greater impact on humanity than any other. Unlike the other "gods" we worship or pray to, only Jesus dealt with the sin problem that has plagued the human race since its inception. Only Jesus left His throne and His divine glory and came down to us in order to save us. Only Jesus took our sins upon Himself and faced God's judgment on sin as a result. Only Jesus was willing to redeem us or "buy us back" from the world of sin that threatens to destroy us. Only Jesus was willing to die for you and for me, so that we may be reconciled to God. And only Jesus is returning to prove it.

We need to grasp this truth now because someday: **Jesus is returning, as the proven Redeemer.**

For over two thousand years, lives have been changed by this one man whose mission it was to leave heaven as God's only Son, come to earth as one of us, and then die for us, because it was the only way to redeem us from our self-destructive behavior.

When He returns in all His glory, all those who have been to the cross and received forgiveness for their sins will be with Him. For everyone else it will be too late. The time of choosing will be over and every tongue will confess and every knee will bow to recognize Jesus Christ as the proven Redeemer—regardless of their background, regardless of their excuses, and regardless of their good intentions.

Jesus is coming to set the record straight:

- He is the only Savior,
- He is the only Redeemer,
- He is the only Messiah, and
- He is the only God.

In the Meantime

Jesus offers those who come to the cross for forgiveness the opportunity to become more and more like Him.

He offers to redeem us from those habits and patterns of behavior that hinder that process.

He offers to redeem us from

- our ignorance and our arrogance;
- our complacency and our indifference;

- our quick tempers and our critical spirits;
- our judgmental attitudes and our appetite for gossip;
- our self-righteousness, self-pity, selfishness, and pride.

Most of all, He offers to redeem us from our refusal to change—so that people know we have been redeemed. This process of change is called sanctification that begins the moment we meet Jesus at the cross and continues until the day we die. Sanctification separates us from the world's way of living and sets us apart for God. It changes us from the inside out. It transforms our thoughts, our desires, our motives, and our actions.

We all pick up baggage in our journey through life. We pack our bags with all sorts of things that can weigh us down: anger, resentment, bitterness, shame, blame, guilt, frustration, disappointment, even despair. And along the way, we can add more weight to our bags of negative traits and emotions: arrogance, pride, stubbornness, insecurity, anxiety, and fear. Our bag becomes heavy and burdensome, and yet we trudge along and even feel justified carrying it—until we meet Jesus. He offers to take it from us and relieve us from the burden. That's how sanctification works. Jesus shows us ever so gently that it is in our best interest to set those heavy bags down and move on without them.

Personal Reflection

I will never forget sitting in a Bible study class as a new student and hearing how this process works. The teacher was using bitterness as an example, not knowing, of course, that was precisely what I was carrying around in my "bag." I listened attentively as she explained how bitterness can actually take root in your soul and basically choke the life right out of you. She admonished us to go home, get on our knees, and give whatever it was we were carrying over to Jesus. I did exactly as she instructed, not even realizing until then how bitter I was that my father had been so AWOL in my life. As soon as I recognized it for what it was and confessed my bitterness before God, it literally began to dissolve. At that point, I was able to forgive my dad and immediately began to love him like I never had before. I got up from my knees feeling happy, relieved, and a whole lot lighter.

145

That's what sanctification does; it unpacks our bags of useless, unnecessary, and even harmful and hurtful items that we gather along the way and repacks them with life-saving alternatives. Sanctification is designed to make us more like Jesus. We are forgiven and, therefore, set free to move forward in Christ, relieved of the baggage we've insisted on carrying. From that point forward, He delights in working with us to make us more like Him. That process of change in my own life enabled me to forgive my father that day and paved the way for the beautiful ending to his life that I was able to share with him.

While Waiting His Return

As we look at our world today, and the evil that is permeating every aspect of our lives, we can't help but wonder how much longer it can continue. The daily news is enough to get our attention and make us realize that time is running out. The world simply cannot continue going in the direction it is going. From genocides to beheadings to nuclear threats and school shootings, the evil around us is rampant and tangible.

But in the midst of the chaos stands the cross.

The cross is God's answer to the wickedness that is spreading faster and is more deadly than the Ebola virus, because only Jesus can change the human heart. He proved it on the cross. The cross provides a new beginning for every single human being. Therefore, only Jesus can swing the tide in our own lives, our families, our schools, our cities, our nation, and the world.

The chorus of this hymn forces us to answer the question we all face at one time or another.

What will you do with Jesus?
Neutral you cannot be.
One day your heart will be asking,
"What will He do with me?"
("What Will You Do with Jesus" by Albert B. Simpson)

Meeting Jesus at the cross settles the matter once and for all.
Have you been there?
How does Jesus' sacrifice for you motivate you to live differently?

146

What is your reaction to the sanctification process?

How will you react to it now, so you can be more like Jesus and make a difference in your world?

This hymn puts it all in perspective.

> When I survey the wondrous cross on which the Prince of
> glory died,
> My richest gain I count but loss, and pour contempt on all my pride.
> Forbid it Lord that I should boast, save in the death of
> Christ, my God;
> All the vain things that charm me most, I sacrifice them to
> His blood.
>
> See, from His head, His hands, His feet, sorrow and love flow
> mingled down;
> Did e'er such love and sorrow meet, or thorns compose so
> rich a crown?
> Were the whole realm of nature mine, that were a present far
> too small;
> Love so amazing, so divine, demands my soul, my life, my all.
> ("When I Survey the Wondrous Cross" by Isaac Watts)

Now let's run to the tomb.

PART III

JESUS CHANGES OUR FUTURE

Chapter 11

Missing at the Tomb
Returning as Life over Death

*N*o one expected the tomb to be empty that first Sunday morning. The disciples should have been there like shoppers at Walmart before Christmas, but they were in hiding for fear the same fate awaited them. The religious leaders were afraid the disciples would steal the body, so they collaborated with Pilate to have Roman soldiers guard the tomb.

Otherwise, life resumed as normal in the city of Jerusalem. Passover was over, so people were back at work, families were back in their routine, markets were open for business. Everything seemed the same, but nothing was the same. Everything was different.

The Promise

God Himself had come down to earth and invited us to know Him and be reconciled to Him, so we could spend eternity with Him. But no one really knew it until the tomb was empty on Sunday morning.

> **Here's the promise:** For believers, the empty tomb means eternal LIFE.

THE EMPTY TOMB

Death no longer has the final say.

The Past

Joseph of Arimathea was a wealthy and prominent member of the Sanhedrin. He and Nicodemus, another member of the Sanhedrin, had contested the council's ruling against Jesus. Nicodemus had come to Jesus secretly at night and learned about being born again (John 3:1-8). He and Joseph must have had many discussions of the Scriptures. Matching prophecies about Jesus must have convinced them He was the Messiah, and therefore, they would expect Him to be sacrificed on the Passover about the same time the lambs were being sacrificed in the temple. And sure enough, He was.

So now Joseph went to Pilate and asked to remove Jesus' body from the cross and bury it in his own private tomb. Pilate couldn't believe Jesus was already dead, so he called for the centurion to confirm it, which he did because he had just given the order to pierce Jesus' side to make sure (John 19:34).

Little did Pilate know that the real Passover Lamb had to die on Passover and that His body could not be left on the cross overnight. But just knowing Jesus was dead put him at ease. So he agreed and granted Joseph permission, but not before issuing an order to seal and guard the tomb, just in case (Mark 15:45; Matthew 27:65-66).

Jewish burial customs dictated that the body be anointed with certain spices and wrapped in linen. So the two men hurried to purchase these supplies before the Day of Preparation for the Sabbath was over. Then they went to Golgotha and removed Jesus from that gruesome cross. What they did was an amazing act of love and confirmation that they believed He was the Messiah and understood the prophecy that He would be buried in a rich man's tomb (Isaiah 53:9). Joseph eagerly stepped up and claimed that privilege for himself.

We can just picture the scene as he and Nicodemus tenderly cleaned Jesus' tortured body, anointed it with seventy-five pounds of myrrh and aloes, and wrapped it in strips of linen (John 19:39-40). There's nothing like making something really dirty clean. Jesus never made Himself dirty; our sins did. Joseph and Nicodemus were acting for all of us down through the ages that have been to the foot of the cross and been forgiven and redeemed by the Savior. We are eternally grateful for this act on our behalf. And we know they must have slept better that night knowing they had made a terrible wrong a little bit right.

Seeing the tomb for myself was everything one could imagine it to be—sacred in the deepest sense of the word. Stooping to go in certainly puts us in the right position.

Once inside, there are burial shelves for two people with a small space to stand and grieve. According to information on my trip, it has been historically proven that only one shelf had been used, making it evident this was more than likely THE tomb.

ENTRANCE TO THE TOMB TODAY

ANOTHER VIEW OF INSIDE

Can you imagine being the first to see it empty? God ordained that three women would have that honor.

The Bible says:

When the Sabbath was over, Mary Magdalene, Mary, the mother of James, and Salome brought spices so that they might go to anoint Jesus' body. Very early on the first day of the week, just after sunrise, they were on their way to the tomb and they asked each other, "Who will roll the stone away from the entrance of the tomb?"

But when they looked up, they saw that the stone, which was very large, had been rolled away. As they entered the tomb, they saw a young man dressed in a white robe sitting on the right side, and they were alarmed.

"Don't be alarmed," he said. "You are looking for Jesus the Nazarene, who was crucified. He has risen! He is not here. See the place where they laid him. But go, tell his disciples and Peter, he is going ahead of you into Galilee. There you will see him just as he told you." (Mark 16:1-7)

Matthew adds:

There was a violent earthquake, for an angel of the Lord came down from heaven and, going to the tomb, rolled back the stone and sat on it. His appearance was like lightning, and his clothes were white as snow. The guards were so afraid of him that they shook and became like dead men. (Matthew 28:2-4)

And Luke tells us that suddenly two men dressed in white were standing beside the women and said:

"Why do you look for the living among the dead? He is not here; He is risen! Remember how he told you while he was still with you in Galilee: 'The Son of Man must be delivered into the hands of sinful men, be crucified and on the third day be raised again.' Then they remembered his words." (Luke 24:5-8)

And John says they ran and got the men.

> Early on the first day of the week, while it was still dark, Mary Magdalene went to the tomb and saw that the stone had been removed from the entrance. So she came running to Simon Peter and the other disciple, the one Jesus loved, and said, "They have taken the Lord out of the tomb, and we don't know where they have put him!"
>
> So Peter and the other disciple started for the tomb. Both were running, but the other disciple outran Peter and reached the tomb first. He bent over and looked in. Then Simon Peter, who was behind him, arrived and went into the tomb. He saw the strips of linen lying there, as well as the burial cloth that had been around Jesus' head. The cloth was folded up by itself, separate from the linen. Finally the other disciple, who had reached the tomb first, also went inside. He saw and believed. (They still did not understand from Scripture that Jesus had to rise from the dead.) (John 20:1-9)

The "stolen body theory," which began with the religious leaders immediately after Jesus died, has persisted down through the centuries with people who do not want to accept the evidence of Jesus' resurrection.

But let's consider these facts:

If someone was going to steal a body, would they bother to unwrap it? If Jesus wasn't really dead, why did the centurion make sure He was by piercing His side, and what convinced him He was the Son of God? If Jesus wasn't the Son of God, why was His death accompanied by so many supernatural signs? What was Pilate afraid of and why did he seal the tomb and post a guard? How was the massive stone rolled away from the grave? Why did the soldiers pass out? What were angels doing there? Why were the disciples hiding? Why didn't they believe?

These questions have been studied by believers and skeptics alike. After all, the bodily resurrection of Jesus Christ remains the convincing proof that He is who He claimed to be—God's Son sent to save the world from sin. But that puts responsibility on the sinner. Do we accept that proof, or do we dig in our heels and resist the salvation

He came to offer because we're just too proud, or too stubborn, or too pre-occupied, or too indifferent?

The writers of the four Gospels give us additional verification and different details surrounding Jesus' resurrection, the most life- and death-changing event in human history. These differences in themselves support the authenticity of the writers' accounts of the resurrection. Written at different times, it's obvious they didn't get together and make sure their accounts matched in every single detail but instead wrote what they remembered, much like we do when thinking back on a major event. We might emphasize one thing, while someone else might emphasize another.

Also, if you were one of the disciples, wouldn't you be embarrassed to admit you didn't really believe Jesus would be raised on the third day even though He had told you over and over again that He would? The fact that His own followers didn't expect His resurrection is another proof that He was resurrected. No one would have dared to make up such a story and be willing to die for it later on.

The bodily resurrection of Jesus Christ is foundational to Christian faith, and yet it remains as much a stumbling block today as it did then. Reactions to this humanly incomprehensible event remain the same, even though the evidence has proven to be irrefutable.

So how can we know for sure?

What would convince us that Jesus really rose from the dead?

Obviously seeing Him with our own eyes, touching Him with our own hands, hearing His voice, and watching Him eat, not just once but over and over so we would know we weren't dreaming, would eventually convince us He was alive. This is exactly how Jesus convinced these frightened, unbelieving, and grieving disciples. He knew their hearts, their fears, their inadequacies, and their lack of faith. So He appeared to them at different times in different settings and with different groups over a period of forty days, so they would believe because they would carry on after Him and pass this information down to us. Their personal accounts are like being there. A few will provide the proof we need to believe as well.

Jesus appeared to the women first.

They had just encountered the angel at the empty tomb who told them to go and tell the disciples—and on the way, suddenly there was Jesus.

The Bible says He said:

> "Greetings! Do not be afraid. Go and tell my brothers to
> go to Galilee; there they will see me." (Matthew 28:9-10)

Imagine Jesus now calling this wimpy band of followers "brothers" after they had deserted Him and Peter had denied Him just as the prophets had foretold and Jesus had warned. And now they were the most reluctant to believe.

But Jesus made sure they would.

Luke records that Jesus appeared to two of the disciples later that day as they were walking to a village called Emmaus. They were discussing this "Breaking News" event in Jerusalem when suddenly— Jesus was walking beside them.

The Bible says He asked:

> "What are you discussing together as you walk along?"
> (Luke 24:17)

With heavy hearts and long faces they proceeded to tell Him everything that had happened. He listened patiently to their hopes that this Jesus would be the one to redeem Israel, but now He was dead (Luke 24:18-24).

The Bible says Jesus replied:

> "How foolish you are, and how slow of heart to believe
> all that the prophets have spoken! Did not the Christ
> have to suffer these things and then enter his glory?"
> (Luke 24:25-26)

For the rest of their journey, Jesus led these two disciples through the Scriptures, beginning with Moses and all the prophets, and explained everything concerning Himself. They were spellbound! As they approached the village, they persuaded Him to stay for dinner.

When He took the bread, gave thanks, broke it, and gave it to them, it dawned on them. This was Jesus! But no sooner had they recognized Him that He disappeared from their sight. They were so excited, they left their meal, hightailed it back to Jerusalem, and went straight to the other disciples and told them (Luke 24:27-33).

In the meantime, Jesus had appeared to Simon Peter (Luke 24:34).

So they all agreed—it was true—Jesus was alive! He had risen from the dead! And suddenly, there He was.

The Bible says **Jesus said:**
"Peace be with you." (Luke 24:36)

But even then, they thought they were seeing a ghost.

So Jesus also said:
"Why are you troubled, and why do doubts rise in your minds? Look at my hands and my feet. It is I myself! Touch me and see; a ghost does not have flesh and bones, as you see I have." (Luke 24:38-39)

We can just imagine the disciples lining up to do just that. But one of them was missing. Thomas would later say, "Unless I see the nail marks in His hands and put my fingers where the nails were, and put my hand into His side, I will not believe it." So a week later, when they were all together behind locked doors, Jesus gave him that opportunity. He suddenly appeared again and went directly over to Thomas (John 20:25-26).

The Bible says **Jesus said:**
"Put your finger here; see my hands. Reach out your hand and put it into my side. Stop doubting and believe." (John 20:27)

How does one even read those words without a deep sense of conviction, because we, too, are slow to believe and quick to doubt. And yet Jesus is patient with us as well and even promises us a greater blessing.

As He told Thomas:

> "Because you have seen me, you have believed; blessed
> are those who have not seen and yet have believed."
> (John 20:29)

But these eleven had the responsibility to spread this news to the world so it would eventually come to us. They had to be thoroughly convinced. So Jesus walked on water, helped them catch a boatload of fish, grilled some on the beach, and then ate it with them, all the time teaching them and preparing them for this task.

Later, Paul reports that Jesus appeared to five hundred people at once (1 Corinthians 15:6). And John tells us that He did many miraculous signs in their presence, which are not even recorded (John 20:30). And we can't help but wonder what else Jesus could have done to convince us to believe He is alive and that when we believe, we will be too, forever. The truth is—nothing! He made sure enough details were accurately recorded to give us ample proof, because He wants people in every generation to know beyond the shadow of a doubt that He has conquered death and therefore, we will too. Now it's up to us to believe, because our future depends on it.

We don't need to fear death, because Jesus proved with the empty tomb that it has lost its power and its hold on us.

The Bible confirms it with these words of comfort:

> Even though I walk through the valley of the shadow of
> death, I will fear no evil, for you are with me; your rod
> and your staff, they comfort me. (Psalm 23:4)

> "Where, O death, is your victory? Where, O death, is your
> sting?" (1 Corinthians 15:55)

> "I tell you the truth, if anyone keeps my word, he will
> never see death." (John 8:51)

The greatest news in the history of the human race is that Jesus Christ is alive, because it means we will live too.

We can be sure this news was traveling all over Israel. And from Israel, it would go to the ends of the earth for the one reason we never want to forget.

The Bible says:
> For God so loved the world that he gave his one and only Son, that whoever believes in him shall not perish but have eternal life. (John 3:16)

We cannot comprehend the love God the Father has for us in sending His Son to this earth to go through all He went through, so we can spend eternity with Him. But the empty grave proves that God accepted Jesus' sacrifice on our behalf, and now Jesus was ready to return to His rightful place by His Father's side in heaven.

When Jesus felt the disciples were ready, He called them all together back in Galilee where He had told them to meet Him. After reinstating Peter as their leader, He left them with this great commission to go out and change the world with the lifesaving news of the salvation He came to offer to all who will receive it. And two thousand years later, people are still being changed by Jesus Christ and then becoming His ambassadors in the world just as He commanded. In the process, this prophecy is being fulfilled.

***The Bible says* Jesus said:**
> "All authority in heaven and on earth has been given to me. Therefore go and make disciples of all nations, baptizing them in the name of the Father and of the Son and of the Holy Spirit, and teaching them to obey everything I have commanded you. And surely I am with you always, to the very end of the age." (Matthew 28:18-20)

Jesus has power over all things:
- all people, all nations, all rulers;

- all circumstances and events;
- all time, space, and history;
- over sin and death and eternity.

But if He had remained on this earth, He would not have been able to fulfill this promise to be with us always. Only His Holy Spirit in His people would make that possible.

So He left His disciples with these final instructions.

The Bible says:

"Do not leave Jerusalem, but wait for the gift my Father promised, which you have heard me speak about. For John baptized with water but in a few days you will be baptized with the Holy Spirit... and you will be my witnesses in Jerusalem, and in all Judea and Samaria and to the ends of the earth." (Acts 1:4-8)

With that, Jesus led the disciples out to the area of Bethany, raised His hands to bless them, and while He was blessing them, was taken up to heaven. All they could do was celebrate! They worshiped Him together and then returned to Jerusalem filled with joy and gratitude. They couldn't stay away from the temple or stop praising God for all they had learned, experienced, and witnessed. Now they were going to have the privilege of sharing it—because the tomb was empty that first Easter morning.

DOOR OVER EMPTY TOMB TODAY

The Future

The empty tomb is cause for great rejoicing because the truth is: **Jesus Christ is returning as life over death.**

No wonder the head cloth was lying by itself in the tomb—neatly folded. According to Jewish tradition, when a master was finished with his meal, he crumpled his napkin and put it on the table for his servant to remove. But when he was coming back, he folded it.

How gracious of Jesus to leave us with such a particular detail. How gracious to let us know beyond the shadow of a doubt that the same power that raised Him from the grave will raise us from ours.

In the Meantime

Many equate Jesus Christ with a Mohammed or a Buddha or a Confucius or a Gandhi or any of the other gods of our own generation. But the fact remains, these gods are dead, and they have stayed dead. And yet we also have the audacity to swear on Jesus' name instead of theirs.

But only Jesus Christ came to us. Only Jesus Christ dealt with the sin problem that condemns us all. Only Jesus Christ died on our behalf. And only Jesus Christ conquered death. So only Jesus Christ is returning to prove it once and for all, because death could not contain Him, and death could not destroy Him, and death could not silence Him.

Personal Reflection

As I think about Jesus' life, death, and resurrection and our own living and dying, I remember these words I quoted at my brother's memorial from an unknown source: "The two most important days of our life are the day we are born and the day we die. The day we are born, only God knows what we will do with our life. The day we die, everyone knows what we did with it. At that point in time, it is public knowledge and our opportunities to change it are over."

It makes me think as humans, we have a need to know that our life matters. The obituaries prove it. We have a need to leave a mark on the world we are leaving behind. So we read the usual:

- date and place of birth
- family background
- educational background
- career achievements
- business awards
- sports endeavors
- club affiliations
- hobbies and pastimes
- world travels
- favorite vacations

INSIDE CHURCH OF THE RESURRECTION TODAY

All of which speak to our lives here on earth, but then what? What are we facing after we die? Jesus' life, ministry, death, and resurrection assure us that life is not over when we die. Death is a mere doorway to a new life—eternal life with Him when we put our faith in Him.

That's why the cross is so powerful. That's why God uses every opportunity, every set of circumstances, and so many people in our lives to draw us to Him, because the cross is, as the Apostle Paul states so beautifully, "the power of God for salvation, for everyone who believes." (Romans 1:16)

As long as we have breath, we can come to the cross and make the necessary changes in our life that will change where we spend eternity.

Perhaps it's a good idea to write our own obituary with this in mind, so we can make the necessary changes and encourage others to do the same. Obituaries are also opportunities to bring attention to God for His working in our life. When we read the occasional "went home to be with the Lord" at the end of one, we can rejoice because that person had it right.

As we think about our own lives and perhaps prepare our own memorial service, these words from the same unknown source I quoted above come to mind: "When we are born, we are crying and everyone around us is smiling; let us live our lives so that when we die, we are smiling and everyone around us is crying—tears of sadness, because they will miss us and the blessing we were in their lives, but also tears of joy, because they look forward to our reunion in heaven." No wonder we're smiling; when our faith is in Jesus Christ, God has a huge "Welcome Home" sign out for us as we pass through "the shadow of death" and meet Him on the other side.

While Waiting His Return

Jesus' resurrection encourages us to believe because it is the only guarantee that we will be resurrected ourselves (John 11:25). Without that guarantee, the pessimists and the atheists would be right. This life would be all there is. But they are so wrong. This life is just for a designated time and a gateway to eternity. The truth is we will all be raised—some to eternal life and some to eternal condemnation (John 3:16-18). So this life is not all there is. It's just a fleeting breath in the face of forever. But Jesus' resurrection proves His power over our greatest enemy and deepest fear, death, and gives us the option to spend that "forever" with Him.

What is your reaction to the empty tomb?

How does it affect the way you think, believe, live, and love?

How will you allow it to prepare you to die, so your time here is not wasted but used to bring others to this life- and death-changing truth?

Easter will never be the same when we are able to sing these words, knowing with absolute certainty that the tomb was empty and ours will be too.

Jesus Christ is risen today…our triumphant holy day,
Who did once upon the cross…suffer to redeem our loss.
Al-le-lu-ia!

Hymns of praise, then let us sing…unto Christ our heavenly King,
Who endured the cross and grave…sinners to redeem and save.
Al-le-lu-ia!

Sing we to our God above…praise eternal as His love.
Praise Him all ye heavenly host…Father, Son and Holy Ghost.
Al-le-lu-ia!
("Jesus Christ is Risen Today" by Charles Wesley)

Now we're ready to go to the Eastern Gate where Jesus will reenter His city as the final proof that He did conquer death, and He's returning to reign as King of kings and Lord of lords.

Chapter 12

Waiting at the Eastern Gate
Returning to Reign as King of Kings and Lord of Lords

$\mathcal{T}$he Old City of Jerusalem is surrounded by a wall with eight gates. Seven allow entry into the city. One has been closed for centuries. The Gate of Mercy, or the Eastern Gate as it is called, is awaiting the return of Jesus Christ.

THE EASTERN GATE TODAY

The Future We Have to Look Forward To
The Old Testament prophet Ezekiel had this vision.

The Bible says:
> Then the man brought me to the gate facing east, and I
> saw the glory of the Lord of Israel coming from the east.
> His voice was like the roar of rushing waters, and the
> land was radiant with his glory. The vision I saw was like
> the vision I had seen when he came to destroy the city
> and like the visions I had seen by the Kebar River, so I
> fell facedown. The glory of the Lord entered the temple
> through the gate facing east. Then the Spirit lifted me up
> and brought me into the inner court, and the glory of the
> Lord filled the temple. (Ezekiel 43:1-5)

There is nothing in our human experience to prepare us for the physical and visible return of Jesus Christ. Scripture alone is our guide and visual aide. Over and over again, Jesus warns us to be ready. The disciples thought He was coming in their lifetime, and every age since has thought the same. But the timing has to be right and the signs in place for the prophecy to be fulfilled. This passage from Ezekiel makes it clear. Jesus will return to His city, Jerusalem, through the Eastern Gate. At that point in time, He will rule the world as King of kings and Lord of lords (1 Timothy 6:13-16; Revelation 19:16).

This is the future we have to look forward to.

This is where all of history is headed.

This is what the Bible points to and describes as the culmination
of this world as we know it.

This is when evil ends and peace reigns on planet Earth.

We've studied the past; let's go right to the future and see how today's events are lining up to fulfill this prophecy.

The question becomes: what has to happen before Jesus returns, and why is there so much hype that it could be any day?

Key indicators are found in Matthew 24. When the disciples asked Jesus when He would return, He gave them a timeline, which, unbeknownst to them, would span at least two thousand years and counting.

The facts are:

* Many false Christs will appear and many people will be deceived.
* There will be wars and rumors of wars.
* Nations will rise against nation and kingdom against kingdom.
* There will be famines and earthquakes in various places.
* Believers will be persecuted and put to death.
* They will be hated by all nations because of their faith.
* Persuasive false prophets will tempt even believers to doubt.
* Wickedness will increase; love will grow cold.
  (Matthew 24:1-12)

This could certainly describe any time frame since Jesus left.

But then, *The Bible says* **Jesus said:**

"This gospel of the kingdom will be preached in the whole world as a testimony to all nations, and then the end will come." (Matthew 24:14)

This is Jesus' highest priority. This is why He came and why He died, and He wants everyone to know it so everyone has an opportunity to respond and be saved.

Has there ever been a time more like now when that could happen? Only our hi-tech capabilities make it possible to reach even the most remote places on earth. So this certainly distinguishes our time from any other, but other prophecies do as well.

There are many, but these three should convince us and prepare us to be ready when Jesus returns: our capacity for knowledge, our capability to destroy, and the nation of Israel.

Our Capacity for Knowledge

Our capacity for knowledge is unparalleled in human history. The Internet has made it possible. Within seconds, we can know almost anything we want to know—from the nearest Mexican restaurant, to the latest research in a particular medical field, to the history of

Christianity from the first to the twenty-first century. We don't even have to be home to access it. Our cell phones and other hi-tech gadgets have become human appendages, so we are in constant communication and have instant access to any information we seek. The Old Testament prophet Daniel described it in the vision he saw of the End Times.

The Bible says:
> "Many will go here and there to increase knowledge."
> (Daniel 12:4)

The problem is that the more we know about the world we live in and our God-given abilities, the less we want to know about the God who created us and blessed us with the ability to know Him, first and foremost. We attribute our success, skills, and achievements to our own making. We pat ourselves on the back and applaud our ingenuity, creativity, and entrepreneurship. Only when we fail and our backs are against the wall, do we stop and reevaluate, and maybe then, look up.

Perhaps that is what Jesus was thinking in His Sermon on the Mount when He said, "Blessed are the meek for they will inherit the earth" (Matthew 5:5). In other words, those who know their rightful position before God will have the right perspective about themselves, the world they live in, and life itself. Everything we have comes from God and everything we have belongs to God. The sooner we realize that the happier we will be, the more content we will be, and the more productive we will be. When we close our eyes in death, nothing goes with us except what we did with and for Jesus Christ. He alone is eternal.

These words were penned long ago by scholar, C.T. Studd:
> "Only one life, 'twill soon be past; only what's done for
> Christ will last."
> (C.T. Studd, "Only One Life")

With that in mind, the questions become:
- What are we doing with all the knowledge available to us today?
- Is it constructive or destructive?

- How are we teaching our children to use the Internet wisely?
- How much time out of our twenty-four-hour day do we give to our "toys"?
- How could we put that time and knowledge to better use?

Our Capability to Destroy

Never before have we had the ability to completely wipe ourselves off the face of the earth. Just the sheer terror of nuclear, biological, and chemical weapons compared to stones, swords, spears, knives, and guns of previous times proves this to be true.

But it was anticipated over two thousand years ago by the prophet Zechariah.

The Bible says:
> Their flesh will rot while they are still standing on their feet, their eyes will rot in their sockets, and their tongues will rot in their mouths. (Zechariah 14:12)

This was unimaginable in Zechariah's day but a very real possibility in ours, thanks to the neutron bomb and other nuclear capability which, at the time of this writing, nine countries have at their disposal and two are seeking. One hasty move by one rogue nation could set in motion the complete annihilation of the human race. So unlike any previous generation, we are capable of destroying all life on planet Earth.

The Nation of Israel

Israel is major proof of God's existence, purpose, plan, power, and sovereignty. Though called the Promised Land because of God's covenant promise to Moses after freeing the Israelites from bondage in Egypt, the people were determined to disobey God and worship other gods besides Him. So God sent a judgment on the land.

The Bible says:
> The whole land will be a burning waste of salt and sulfur—nothing planted, nothing sprouting, no vegetation growing on it. It will be like the destruction of

Sodom and Gomorrah, Admah and Zeboiim, which the Lord overthrew in fierce anger. All the nations will ask: "Why has the Lord done this to this land? Why this fierce, burning anger?"

And the answer will be: "It is because this people abandoned the covenant of the Lord, the God of their fathers, the covenant he made with them when he brought them out of Egypt. They went off and worshiped other gods and bowed down to them, gods they did not know, gods he had not given them. Therefore the Lord's anger burned against this land, so he brought on it all the curses written in this book. In furious anger and great wrath the Lord uprooted them from their land and thrust them into another land, as it is now." (Deuteronomy 29:23-28)

And so it was that Israel as a nation was dispersed for hundreds of years. But God keeps His promises, and the prophet Ezekiel foresaw the day when He would bring His people home. Not because of anything they did to deserve it, but because of His covenant with them and purpose through them.

The Bible says:

This is what the sovereign Lord says: "It is not for your sake, O house of Israel, that I am going to do these things, but for the sake of my holy name, which you have profaned among the nations where you have gone. I will show the holiness of my great name, which has been profaned among the nations, the name you have profaned among them. Then the nations will know that I am the Lord, declares the Sovereign Lord, when I show myself holy through you before their eyes. For I will take you out of the nations; I will gather you from all the countries and bring you back into your own land." (Ezekiel 36:22-24)

On May 14, 1948, Israel became a nation, and her people began streaming home from all corners of the earth just as the prophet

Isaiah had foretold (Isaiah 11:11-12). This is unprecedented in human history. Never before had a people been scattered all over the globe only to be regathered again. They came from everywhere. As prophesied by Isaiah and Jeremiah, they came from the north, south, east and west—from Europe, Asia, Africa, North and South America.

And more prophecies were fulfilled, as the nation was transformed from a wasteland to a lush and prosperous land that exports millions of dollars of fresh produce, flowers, plants, wine, and other goods each year (Isaiah 35:1). This prosperity was inconceivable only a century ago, showing us that God is on the throne controlling all people, nations, rulers, and events according to His perfect will and purpose. And Israel is at the center of that purpose.

So other prophecies became reality:

- Jerusalem would be rebuilt on its own ruins—and it is.
- Jerusalem would be trampled on by Gentiles (non-Jews)— and it was until 1967.
- Jews would be persecuted—and they have, more than any other people on earth.
- Surrounding nations would unite against Israel—and they have.
- Israel would be invincible—wars have not destroyed her.
- Israel will remain God's chosen people—and she is.
- The Eastern Gate would remain closed until the Messiah comes—and it is.
- The returning Jews would have no king until Jesus returns— and they don't.
- The temple would be rebuilt—it's in the works.
- Temple sacrifices would be reestablished—stay tuned.
  Scripture references: Jeremiah 30:18; Luke 21:24; Jeremiah 29:18; Psalm 83:4-8; Zechariah 12:6-9; Joel 3:2; Ezekiel 44:1-3; Hosea 3:4-5; 2 Thessalonians 2:3-4; Daniel 9:27.

But many other prophecies indicate we are in the End Times as well. For example, these certainly resonate: increased violence and deadly disease (Luke 21:10-11); extreme weather and environmental devastation (Luke 21:25-26; Revelation 11:18). We also see flagrant sexual sin, spiritual rebellion, a false gospel being preached, and people being "lovers of themselves" (Genesis 19; Romans 1:24-27;

Revelation 9:21; 2 Peter 2:1-3; 2 Timothy 3:1-2). On the global front, we see movement toward a one-world religion and a global economic system (Revelation 13:8, 12, 16-17). The fact we can Google all these topics and get hundreds of hits shows how clearly our times reflect the description of the End Times.

In the midst of this environment, we see how a world desperate for peace is ripe for a world leader as prophesied in Daniel 8:23-25 and Revelation 13:16-18. Yet against all odds, the Word of God will survive (Luke 21:33).

Fulfillment of these prophecies would lead up to a time of unprecedented suffering for mankind. Jesus likened it to the days of Noah before the flood—a time of extreme wickedness, sexual immorality, and rebellion against God. We cannot ignore the similarities.

Sitting on the Mount of Olives with His disciples a few days before His death, Jesus describes this time.

The Bible says:
> "There will be great distress, unequaled from the beginning of the world until now—and never to be equaled again." (Matthew 24:21)

It is rightly called the Tribulation. It is the last seven years of history as we know it, just before Jesus returns to earth. In the middle of the seven years, or after three and one-half years, the archenemy of Jesus Christ, known as the Antichrist because he opposes everything about Christ, will reveal his true identity by going into the rebuilt temple in Jerusalem and demand to be worshiped. This is known as the "abomination that causes desolation" that is recorded for us in Matthew 24:15 (Daniel 9:27).

By the time that happens, this evil ruler will be in control of the world. His promise to bring peace, when nations are desperate for peace, will be his ticket to power. His charisma, oratory, and Satan-appointed authority will give him control of governments, economics, and religion. In fact, no one will even be able to buy groceries or do business without the required "mark" on their hand or forehead (Revelation 13:17).

Again, this has never been possible before now. But a simple microchip implanted under our skin would suffice. Defying his leadership and refusing to worship him as God will not be an option, unless you want to die. His main goal will be to utterly destroy Israel once and for all, so he summons all nations for the ultimate and final battle on planet Earth. It is called the Battle of Armageddon (Revelation 16:16), and it is the most studied battle or series of battles ever fought that hasn't yet been fought. But the clock is ticking and the players are maneuvering for position.

It is incomprehensible that the nations will come against God's people in utter defiance of Jesus Christ and actually think that their numbers, weapons, and power can destroy His people and His land. But they do. And in their arrogance, they assume success is inevitable. After all, what is tiny Israel against so many?

But oh, how we underestimate God! The Old Testament prophet Joel tells us that God Himself will gather the nations together in this one place for one reason—to be judged.

The Bible says:
"I will gather all nations and bring them down to the Valley of Jehoshaphat. There I will enter into judgment against them concerning my inheritance, my people Israel,…" (Joel 3:2)

And so they come. And just when it is certain Israel will be "wiped off the face of the earth," the nations are stopped in their tracks by the visible and unmistakable power of Almighty God.

The Bible says:
Immediately after the distress of those days "the sun will be darkened, and the moon will not give its light; the stars will fall from the sky, and the heavenly bodies will be shaken."
At that time the sign of the Son of Man will appear in the sky, and all the nations of the earth will mourn. They will see the Son of Man coming on the clouds of the sky, with power and great glory. And he will send his angels with a loud trumpet call, and they will gather his elect

from the four winds, from one end of the heavens to the other. (Matthew 24:29-31)

God's army will intervene to save His people.

Late in the first century, the Apostle John had this vision while he was exiled on Patmos for spreading the truth about Jesus Christ to the known world. God told him to write down what he saw, and then He made sure it was preserved for all time, so we'll know the end of the story.

The Bible says:

I saw heaven standing open and there before me was a white horse, whose rider is called Faithful and True. With justice he judges and makes war. His eyes are like blazing fire, and on his head are many crowns. He has a name written on him that no one knows but he himself. He is dressed in a robe dipped in blood, and his name is the Word of God. The armies of heaven were following him, riding on white horses and dressed in fine linen, white and clean. Out of his mouth comes a sharp sword with which to strike down the nations. "He will rule them with an iron scepter." He treads the winepress of the fury of the wrath of God Almighty. On his robe and on his thigh he has this name written: KING OF KINGS AND LORD OF LORDS. (Revelation 19:11-16)

Who can stand against the wrath of Almighty God, His justified anger, and judgment against sin? No one! The nations will be defeated and the blood of millions will literally cover the land, and birds of prey will come and devour their flesh (Revelation 19:21). In the face of such near extinction, the Jews will finally recognize their Messiah and mourn for Him like a parent mourns their only child (Zechariah 12:10).

As Jesus spoke these words to His disciples on the Mount of Olives, they must have been sitting on the edge of their seats. Who could contain themselves? Jesus knew their thoughts.

The Bible says **He said:**

> "Learn this lesson from the fig tree. As soon as its twigs get tender and its leaves come out, you know that summer is near. Even so, when you see all these things, you know that it is near, right at the door. I tell you the truth, this generation will certainly not pass away until all these things have happened. Heaven and earth will pass away, but my words will never pass away." (Matthew 24:32-35)

In a world that is shaken with uncertainty, insecurity, and fear, these words should motivate us to open our Bibles and give God at least the same attention we give "Good Morning America" or the nightly news. He has seen to it that we don't have to go through this life in fear and trembling because of what is happening in our world. Instead we can know that He knows all things, planned all things, and is in control of all things.

The Bible is one-third prophecy, which means it foretells future events under God's divine and inspired leading. Therefore, it is accurate and inerrant. We can count on God when we cannot count on anyone or anything else, even taking our next breath. He has graciously provided His written Word for us to learn from and live by. We can know what the future holds. We just don't know when it will unfold and for good reason, because Jesus wants every generation to be ready when He returns.

But one generation will have the advantage over all others because the signs will be clear; the time is near, even right at the door. The key is the establishment of Israel as a nation in 1948. Everything else falls in line behind that one date. At this writing, that is exactly sixty-six years ago. Could this be the generation?

So we have to ask ourselves:

How can we ignore the signs today?

Why would we want to?

And yet Jesus is quick to clarify that no one knows the day or the hour, not even Him, only the Father (Matthew 24:36). But that is all the more reason to be ready, so He says, stay awake, pay attention, be alert, keep watch, because it will happen when you least expect it.

177

In other words, He is not going to text us and say, "Today's the day I'm coming; my ETA is 12 noon!"

So every day should be lived expecting Him to and hoping He will because the truth is: **Jesus is returning to reign as KING of kings and LORD of lords!**

Think of it! The most amazing event in human history won't take place in a giant stadium in Melbourne or Los Angeles or New York or Rome or Athens or Sochi or Beijing, nor will it be confined to prime-time TV. It will be live coverage, visible from every speck of land on earth. There will be no place it will not be seen, and every creature on earth will have front row seats.

Jesus will come down here just as He left here two thousand years ago. His feet will stand on the Mount of Olives and the sheer power of His arrival will cause it to split in two (Zechariah 14:4). He will charge through the Eastern Gate to enter His city, Jerusalem, with His people—believers from every age, culture, race, language, and nationality. And there He will reign, and this world will be brought under His Kingship. Nations will come and honor Him. Peace will prevail, and the wolf will lay down with the lamb (Isaiah 11:6).

Jerusalem will get a heavenly makeover. The New Jerusalem will be a sight to behold. It will literally be heaven on earth.

Again, the Apostle John received the preview.

The Bible says **he saw:**
> The Holy City, Jerusalem coming down out of heaven from God. It shone with the glory of God, and its brilliance was like that of a very precious jewel, like a jasper, clear as crystal. It had a great high wall with twelve gates, and with twelve angels at the gates. On the gates were written the twelve tribes of Israel. There were three gates on the east, three on the north, three on the south and three on the west. The wall of the city had twelve foundations, and on them were the names of the twelve apostles of the Lamb. (Revelation 21:10-14)

God is the perfect architect, and He has planned everything from the very beginning. He formed the nation of Israel from the twelve tribes of Israel to be the vehicle through which the Messiah would come and His Word would be preserved. Each tribe will be honored with a Gate in the New Jerusalem. From these twelve tribes He called twelve men to follow Him and be His disciples while on earth. After Jesus' resurrection, Matthias would replace Judas Iscariot and these twelve disciples would become the twelve apostles, sent out by God to initiate His rescue mission and spread the good news of His salvation to the world. Their names will be forever remembered on the twelve foundations stones of the wall surrounding the New Jerusalem.

But the temple is gone because Jesus, the Lord God Almighty and the Lamb, are the temple. And the city doesn't need the sun or the moon because Jesus, the Light of the world, is there. The gates will never be shut. And only those whose names are written in the Lamb's book of life may enter. God's throne will be in the center and a river will flow from it to water the tree of life (Revelation 21:22-22:2)—a river like the River Jordan where Jesus' ministry to mankind began and a tree of life like the tree of life in the Garden of Eden where our need for Him began.

And so we have a sweeping history of God's redemptive plan for the human race. What began in Genesis with the promise of a Messiah, the anointed One, the Savior who would come and save us from our sins, ends in Revelation when He returns to reign.
It is only fitting that Jesus leaves us with these words.

The Bible says He said:
"Behold, I am coming soon! My reward is with me, and I will give to everyone according to what he has done. I am the Alpha and the Omega, the First and the Last, the Beginning and the End. Blessed are those who wash their robes, that they may have the right to the tree of life and may go through the gates into the city." (Revelation 22:12-14)

"Yes, I am coming soon." (Revelation 22:20)

Are you ready?

Jesus could come for believers any minute. Many believe (myself included) that will usher in the seven years of tribulation which will end with His return to earth. Everything is in place for that to happen.

My older brother was often left in charge of us four younger siblings when our parents went to the horse races. He would let us have our fun and freedom during the day but come five o'clock, he'd say, "hurry up. Get the house in order. They're coming!"

Jesus is coming and all the signs indicate—soon!

After seven centuries of being closed, the Eastern Gate will open for the King of Glory to enter and prove to all creation that He is the King of kings and the Lord of lords.

ANOTHER VIEW OF THE EASTERN GATE

What are we to do in the meantime?

How should we live?

We should live like we believe it, because when we believe that Jesus Christ is God and that He came to this earth the first time to save us from our sins and that He is returning to prove it, we will live differently than we have ever lived before. We will trust His love for us, we will trust His will for us, we will trust His provision for us and therefore, we will live with a new sense of purpose and security. Our contentment, our hope, and our joy will no longer be in ourselves or depend on our circumstances but in the one and only eternal God, our Lord and Savior Jesus Christ. We will live for Him and for His glory. And when He comes, we will be glad we did.

The Bible says:

Lift up your heads, O you gates, be lifted up, you ancient doors, That the King of glory may come in. Who is this King of Glory? The Lord strong and mighty, the Lord mighty in battle.

Lift up your heads O you gates, lift them up, you ancient doors, That the King of glory may come in. Who is he, this King of glory? The Lord Almighty—he is the King of glory. (Psalm 24:7-10)

Come, Lord Jesus, come quickly!
Amen.

Dear Reader,

Every day the news is confirming the direction our world is going. Every day the signs of Jesus' return as presented in this book are becoming more realistic, relevant, and recognizable.

At this writing, terrorism is increasing around the world; the Islamic terrorist group ISIS and other jihadists groups are penetrating the world's major cities, even recruiting young Americans in America to kill Americans; the United States is distancing itself from Israel, making her more isolated and vulnerable to the enemies around her; the Prime Minister of Israel is inviting Jews around the world to come home; Iran continues its relentless pursuit of nuclear weapons despite UN pressure and the threat to world peace.

In the midst of this chaos, the Word of God stands firm and unchanging. His promises are true. We can count on Him to give us hope, security, and peace now, and we can know that He is coming again to secure our future with Him forever, when we put our faith in Him.

Every day our time on this earth as we know it is getting shorter and our opportunity to know Jesus Christ as the fulfillment of these promises we have studied is drawing to a close.

As you close this book, it is my prayer that you have made the choice to give your life and your future to Him. If you haven't, I urge you to do so now because at the end of your life, nothing is more important and nothing else matters—and no one wants to learn that too late.

Candace Brown Doud
March 2015

ACKNOWLEDGEMENTS

*W*ithout the solid foundation of sound Biblical teaching, this book could never have been written. Studying the Bible brings us face-to-face with our need for Jesus Christ and God's plan for our life. I am eternally grateful to Bible Study Fellowship International, a worldwide teaching ministry, for their commitment to excellence in this regard. As a class member, then in leadership, and later as a Teaching Leader, the knowledge and training I received through this organization was, and continues to be, life-changing.

To Jim, my husband of fifty-two years, who has supported me one hundred percent—first, as I *finally* became a student, then a teacher, and now a writer. This book would not be going to print without you. Thank you for all the "morning briefings" to fill me in on world events that continue to confirm the timing of this book. Thank you for the freedom and encouragement to pursue and persevere.

To Julie Painley who told me, "You have a book in you" even though you had never met me personally. You helped me take on this "assignment" with obedience and confidence.

To Linda Wagner who became the "coach" to bring it to completion. Your professional expertise and gentle prodding helped me not be satisfied with anything less than my best effort. I am forever changed and grateful for knowing you and learning from you.

To Debbie Austin, a real pro at copyediting. You patiently added the necessary final touches.

To my "prayer team" who prayed me through developing the content of the book. Through your prayers and encouragement, I was inspired to keep on keeping on.

To my "readers" whose valuable feedback helped fine-tune the material.

To my pastor, Dr. Scott Dudley, a huge thanks for your interest and helpful suggestions.

To my family: my late brother, David, a dynamic example of faith and perseverance; my brother, Steven, and sisters, Robbin and Victoria, the bond we share is motivating and priceless; my granddaughter, Brooke, for making the trip to Israel with me and taking all the beautiful pictures; my granddaughter, Tate, for your multi-talents and always cheering me on; my grandson, Daniel, for your literary talent and technical support. And to my children, your spouses, and my younger seven grandchildren, with so much love and gratitude for your love and support. We have been given the great privilege of carrying the torch of faith forward to the next generation and to the next after that. May we be committed to that task because, in the end, nothing else matters.

Most of all, thank you, Lord Jesus, for the privilege of this "assignment" and all this support I needed to complete it. It is for Your honor and glory.

CPSIA information can be obtained at www.ICGtesting.com
Printed in the USA
LVOW02s1008260915

455852LV00012B/278/P